Testimonials for Countdown to Easter

Countdown to Easter holds a wealth of treasures waiting for families to discover! Amy has a gift for uncovering delightful stories and activities from the past, combining them with project ideas of her own, and sharing them with others. This book is full of little-known stories, fun activities, recipes, and crafts that will bring families closer together and closer to the risen Savior. It is a wonderful tool that can be used to make Easter the beautiful, meaningful remembrance it should be.

    Mary Evelyn Notgrass, www.notgrass.com
    www.christianmusicaltheatre.com

Amy Puetz has once again delivered an excellent book in *Countdown to Easter*. This incredible collection of stories, songs, poems and activities will guide you through the week leading up to Easter and make each day very special. Amy has great talent and passion for making events from the past come alive in this present day. These talents, combined with and complimented by, her wonderful love for the Lord make this book a must read!

    Lisa Williams, author of *A Poetic Journey*
    http://joyfuljourney.christianblogsites.com/blog

This is more than a 'countdown,' it's a fully involved inter-active resource that will clearly point your family to Jesus. Thank you Amy for "Beefing Up" the Easter celebration and making it fun!

    Patrick Herman-Music Director, **Pilgrim Radio Network**

Countdown to EASTER

Countdown to EASTER

By Amy Puetz

Memory Making Stories & Activities for 14 Days Leading up to Easter

*To people everywhere who have
found the true meaning of Easter!*

Copyright 2010 by Amy Puetz
All Rights Reserved.

No part of this book may be reproduced in any form or by any electronic or mechanical means including information storage and retrieval systems, without permission in writing from the author. The only exception is by a reviewer, who may quote short excerpts in a review.

Published by Golden Prairie Press
P.O. Box 429; Wright, WY 82732
www.AmyPuetz.com

Cover & Layout Design - Amy Puetz

All of the quotes, poems, riddles, songs, and classic stories in this book were published before 1923 and are in the public domain. Even though the stories themselves are in the public domain this anthology is copyrighted.

ISBN: 978-0-9825199-2-9

LCCN: 2010921044

Library of Congress Cataloging-in-Publication Data

Includes index.
I. 1. Classic Stories. 2. Easter—Crafts. 3. Easter Eggs—Games. 4. Riddles. 5. Easter Songs.
II. Title

Contents

Introduction..1
Monday Before Palm Sunday...........................2
"Finding Easter" by Carolyn Sherwin Bailey 3, Easter Chuckles by Melville De Lancey Landon & Mark Twain 5, Easter Craft—Easter Cards by Lina Beard and Adelia Belle Beard 6, "Luther's Easter Hymn" 7
Tuesday Before Palm Sunday...........................8
"Easter Eggs" Part 1 by Christoph Von Schmid 9, Cooking—Matzo Bread by Amy Puetz 13
Wednesday Before Palm Sunday..................14
"Easter Eggs" Part 2 by Christoph Von Schmid 15, "Easter Hymn" by Charles Wesley 18, Easter Quiz—The Easter Story by Amy Puetz 19
Thursday Before Palm Sunday.......................20
"Playmates in Egypt" by Elma Ehrlich Levinger 21, "Easter Carol" by George Newell Lovejoy 22, Easter Craft—Wall Hanging - History of the Passover by Amy Puetz 23, An Egg-speriment To Put an Egg in a Glass Bottle by Melville De Lancey Landon & Mark Twain 23
Friday Before Palm Sunday............................27
"Harold's Happy Easter" 28 & "The Wonder Egg" 29 by Carolyn Sherwin Bailey, What is Easter? by William Tegg 29, Easter Craft—Easter Baskets 30
Saturday Before Palm Sunday........................31
"Love Triumphant" by Florence Morse Kingsley 32, "The Shadow of the Cross" by Horatius Bonar 34, Easter Songs—"Alas! And Did My Savior Bleed?" 35, "Near the Cross" 36
Palm Sunday..37
"An Easter Snow Storm" Part 1 by P. Kitty Koudacheff 38, "The Splendor of the Lilies" by Margaret Elizabeth Munson Sangster 40, Easter Riddles by Melville De Lancey Landon & Mark Twain 41, Easter Craft—Easter Bookmarks by Amy Puetz 41, "How a Little Brown Bulb Became an Easter Lily" by Florence Ursula Palmer 43
Monday - Passion Week.................................44
"An Easter Snow Storm" Part 2 by P. Kitty Koudacheff 45, "The Two Thieves" by Mrs. Jameson 47, Cooking—Decorate Easter Eggs by Amy Puetz 48
Tuesday - Passion Week.................................49
"A Lesson of Faith" by Mrs. Julia Cowles 50, Easter Egg Activities—Easter Egg Hunt & The Celebration of Easter by Ellye Howell Glover 52, Easter Egg Games by Lina Beard & Adelia Belle Beard 53
Wednesday - Passion Week............................55
"The Nazarene" by Lew Wallace 56, Easter Party—Easter Hat Sale and Hoop Race for Easter by Ellye Howell Glover 61
Thursday - Passion Week................................62
"The Healer" by Lew Wallace 63, Easter Songs—"When I Survey the Wondrous Cross" 67, "Beneath the Cross of Jesus" 68
Passover - Good Friday..................................69
"Miss Rebecca's Easter Blossoms" by Harriet A. Nash 70, Legend of The Nails 73, Cooking—Hot Cross Buns by Amy Puetz 74
Saturday Before Easter..................................75
"The General's Easter Box" by Temple Bailey 76, "Jesus Christ is Risen Today" Author Unknown 80, Easter Quiz—Who Said It? by Amy Puetz 81
Easter - Resurrection Sunday.........................82
"The Loveliest Rose in the World" by Hans Christian Andersen 83, "Easter Poem" by Caleb Davis Bradlee 84, Easter Songs—"All Hail the Power" 85, "Christ the Lord Is Risen Today" 86
Index..87

Introduction

It is my sincere wish that this book will be used to create wonderful memories for you and your family. In our society there are so many things that vie for our attention that we often don't spend time with those we love most. A hundred years ago things were very different. Families would spend time in the evenings talking, reading, singing, and just fellowshipping. With the creation of the radio things changed and when television became a staple in every home the interaction between family members decreased even more. Now with computers, movies, and a myriad of other gadgets, families spend very little time building relationships. This book has a mission to help families grow closer together.

Before you jump into this book I have a few things I'd like to say. The book is broken up into daily sections. Each day has a story and an activity that should take about 30 to 45 minutes to go through. The story is first but feel free to change it around and start with the activity if it works best for you. Some of the activities, such as cooking, may take more than the allotted time, so preview the activity before you get started. For instance, on the Monday before Easter there are instructions for making Easter eggs, which could take quite a while. You might start making the hard boiled eggs and read the story while the eggs are cooking. Also if one of the activities doesn't sound like it will suit your family, feel free to implement your own. If you have a special recipe you make every year, do this on a cooking day; or if you have a craft that you enjoy, do that on a craft day. Most people have a tradition of when they make Easter eggs and have an egg hunt. I've put them on the Monday and Tuesday before Easter, but they could be done at anytime.

Nearly all the stories in this book were written in the 1800s and early 1900s so some of the language may seem old fashioned, but this only adds to their charm. I have modernized some of the spelling but I left most of the stories intact because the Victorian people had such a beautiful way of using words. It is always good to stretch our own vocabulary. Many of these stories have not been reprinted since their first publication and I'm so excited to share these with a whole new generation. Most of the stories can be used to help teach children important lessons. At the end of each story you could think of a few questions to ask your children, or maybe even have the children ask you questions! For instance, on the Wednesday before Palm Sunday you could ask, "How did an act of kindness bring lost ones together?" You could also have the children look up Bible verses that talk about a virtue that was mentioned in the story. On the Monday before Palm Sunday you could look up "giving" in a concordance and read a few passages. There are lots of different ways that you can make this experience more meaningful for your family. Just make sure that you have fun!

Thank you for taking the time to read this introduction and I pray that your family will grow closer to each other and to God during this Easter season.

Have a Happy Easter,
Amy Puetz

Countdown to Easter

Monday Before Palm Sunday

Finding Easter
By Carolyn Sherwin Bailey

The girls in Miss Janeway's class flocked out of Sunday school together, chattering like the first robins that could be heard in the orchard back of the church.

"Did you see that lovely flowered ribbon in the window of the millinery shop?" Janet Graham exclaimed. "I am going to ask mother if I can't have my Easter hat trimmed with it."

"They have ever so many new flowers too," Molly Arnold broke in, "little bunches of artificial wild flowers, and wreaths of daisies and sprays of lilacs. I want a white leghorn hat trimmed with lilacs. I think it is such a nice fashion to have a new hat for Easter. It makes one feel just like the spring, all dressed up new for Easter Day. That is what Miss Janeway spoke of today in class, wasn't it? She said we were to think of Easter as the time when the old things were made new."

Janet considered a minute. "Yes, I know she said that," she assented. "It seemed strange to me though, for Miss Janeway never does seem to think very much about getting new clothes for special occasions. She's going to wear her blue serge suit and her winter hat for the Easter service even if she could have silk and satin if she wanted them." Janet puckered her forehead into a puzzled frown as she spoke, but just then Miss Janeway appeared in the chapel door and the girls rushed over to crowd around her.

She was not much more than a girl herself, the daughter of the rector, and fresh from college. She was full of the rare charm that comes from forgetfulness of self, and her plain clothes only served to enhance the slender grace of her figure, the soft glints of her simply coiled brown hair, and the lights of her deep hazel eyes. She made blue serge take on the regal lines of velvet through the charm of her own winning personality. No wonder her class in Sunday school loved her. She walked toward the street, the girls flocking to her like a swarm of bees flying about a flower.

"I heard what you were talking about," she said, laughingly. "You are all going to blossom out Easter Sunday like a garden. Of course you will look very pretty; but what, for instance, is the need of Janet's covering up her lovely hair with all that ribbon she is thinking of having on her new hat? And Molly doesn't need blue lilacs, for her eyes are just that color. Do you know, girls, I have just loved those tam-o'-shanter caps like your coats that you have worn lately; they look so simple and girlish. Easter comes early this year, and you could just as well wear them a little longer," she finished, persuasively.

Hope Dunbar looked up timidly now, a flush of excitement lighting her pale little face. There had been hard times at Dr. Dunbar's since he had been called to service in the army and left Hope and her mother with very little to keep the home until his return. Hope touched Miss Janeway's arm. "I think that is such a sweet thought of yours," she said, "but everyone does always wear something new for Easter. You spoke about it in class today. You said, 'The old things shall be made new.'"

Miss Janeway's face lighted in the way that the girls always said made her look like one of the church window angels. She seemed to be looking far off as she spoke.

"Yes, that's what Easter means," she said, softly—"old branches living again in apple blossoms, and buried bulbs sending up crocuses and tulips and Easter lilies, and dead hearts living again in faith—and the resurrection. Don't you see, girls? We've had the wrong idea about it for ever so long."

They had reached the gate of the rectory now and Miss Janeway turned to the members of the class who were still about her.

"Come in, and let me make you some tea," she said. "I want to talk things over with you and see if we can't plan an Easter different from any that we have ever had here in Maywood."

Grouped around the open fire in the living room, and enjoying tea and crisp toast and strawberry jam from dainty rosebud china, the girls talked, and began to understand, and made plans.

"There's ever so much that's old in my house that I can make over, just by helping," Hope said. "I don't mean the carpets and the paint, for that would take money, but mother's old worries about how she was going to get anything new for me for Easter. I shall just tell her that I am not going to have a new hat. And there is her backache from doing all the housework since we have had to get along without a maid. I didn't think I could spare the time from my school homework to do the dishes, but I will, and iron, and dust, and make the beds too." Hope ended with an energetic nod of her curly head.

Miss Janeway put her arm around the little girl and drew her close to her. "I think that will be a most beautiful way, to make Easter blossom in a house," she said. "No new things could be better than thoughtfulness and loving helpfulness. Now, girls, I leave it all to you," she said as the early spring sunset lighted the windows, and it was time for them to go. "Tell the others and go to work every one of you, to see how much you can find in this town to make new for Easter."

It was such a different way of thinking about Easter that the girls forgot all about their clothes, except that those who were to have had new ones obtained permission to use the money their mothers would have spent to help out the wonderful plan. They held meetings at their different homes after school and on Saturdays, and Maywood began to be surprised into a new kind of blooming, different from that of its orchards, and lawns, and hedges.

Hope's example was such a good one that those of the girls who found the need, and there were a good many, tried to bring about some Easter blossoming in their own homes.

"Mother hasn't had a new dress in a year," one girl confided to Hope. "She always gets something pretty for me instead, but I am just making her buy cloth for a dress, and I know I can help her make it."

Window boxes appeared to make the fronts of bare houses more attractive. The girls raked the dead leaves from lawns, set out plants, cleaned up rubbish in the schoolyard and in the park, and a few very courageous ones painted their front fences. Janet, Molly, and Miss Janeway took the leadership of the movement and tried to discover special kinds of Easter service that the girls could do. More than Miss Janeway's special class had become interested, so there was quite a group of girls to draw upon.

"The books in the Sunday school library do look so badly," Miss Janeway said one day. "The covers are torn and soiled. The new covers have come, but no one seems to have any time to take off the old ones and put on the new."

"We'll do it Monday afternoon," Hope decided, "instead of having our regular basketball practice." And they did. When the many hands had finished, the library was fresh and neat for Easter. The rows of cleanly covered books lent a distinctive brightness to the room where they were kept.

"I went by the hospital today," Janet said, "and so many children were looking out of the windows in the children's ward. They are the getting-better, but not-well kiddies, and, just think, they will have to stay there over Easter." She thought a moment. Then she spoke eagerly: "We girls could go and tell stories in the children's ward on visiting days, and keep it up all the spring," she exclaimed. "That would be something new and different for them."

The story hour in the hospital worked wonders. When small Peter, who had been in bed for weeks with a fractured leg, heard the story of the Little Lame Prince and realized what patience in pain can work, he began to gain.

"I don't know what's come over Peter," the nurse in the ward said to Janet one afternoon as she was leaving with her fairy books. "He's so good and so quiet."

"I know," Janet said. "He's spending his days 'way up in the clouds on a magic carpet, instead of in bed, and so he doesn't feel his splints and he's getting well faster."

It was quite true, and the same miracle thing happened to the other children. They left the ashes of their everyday suffering with Cinderella and danced with her at the ball whose joy was a veritable tonic to them. Stories of outdoors, stories of adventure, and stories of achievement helped the little convalescents to see the good, new things that awaited them when they should be well enough to leave the hospital. And the vision helped them to get well faster. The girls enjoyed the story hour as much as the children. They had never realized before how a beautiful story could make the one who heard it see life with a new vision.

Molly discovered the last work for the girls.

"Old Mr. Burns, who has the greenhouse, is so worried about his Easter trade," she told the girls about ten days before Easter. "He lost all his help when the men enlisted and he can't get anyone to help him. He says that he depends so much on the money he makes selling Easter plants to keep the greenhouse going the rest of the year."

"We'll help him," Janet announced.

So the girls put on their Camp Fire suits and went to Mr. Burns's assistance for every afternoon of the week before Easter. It seemed the happy climax to all their efforts as they worked in the rich, earth-smelling loam, and listened to the old man's homely philosophy about his growing things.

"There couldn't be anything much more discouraging looking than a rosebush shoot when you first start it," he said, "or a lily bulb. But all they need is a little encouragement, and the first thing you know you have roses and lilies." His words made the Easter message come true for the girls. Every year the earth, right there in their own town, was holding and cherishing old things, and sending them up new.

The girls washed flowerpots, and carefully potted tulips, hyacinths, and daffodils under the old florist's direction. As Easter drew near they cut great, odorous violets and bunched them in soft paper in boxes. They delivered the potted and cut flowers, and passed and repassed the milliner's window countless times without once thinking of the artificial flowers there, ready for Easter hats.

It had been the happiest Easter season that they had ever known. Then it was Easter itself, come on birds' wings through blue skies, before they knew it. Not one was ready for the day as they always had been before with new frocks, shoes, ribbons, and gloves. Each girl in Miss Janeway's class was prepared, though, in a new way. Hope Dunbar put this into words as they all met in the choir room before they marched into church for the Easter service.

"How nice we all look in our old things!" she exclaimed. "I feel Easter so that it really seems as if I am really dressed up for it."

The light shining in through the colored windows, the sweet odor of the flowers that banked the church, and the music that rang out with Easter joy and faith seemed more beautiful than at any Easter service before. There were so many flowers too—a bewildering profusion of color—massed at the front of the church. Old Mr. Burns, dressed in a neatly brushed black suit, sat in one of the front pews, and the girls had seen him talking to Miss Janeway before they marched in. They both looked mysterious and happy. When the service was over, the girls discovered the reason. As they filed out, the old florist took his place by the flowers and gave each girl a pot of Easter blossoms to take home.

It was part his offering, and part Miss Janeway's. As the girls went out, almost hidden by the tall lilies, bright geraniums, and purple hyacinths and heliotrope, they made a happy Easter pageant of bloom and beauty. Janet pulled her old cap down over her braids as a puff of wind met her at the door. She hugged her pot of geraniums tighter.

"Who wants an Easter hat," she laughed, "when they can have Easter this way?"

Easter Chuckles! By Melville De Lancey Landon and Mark Twain

Ethel, when she was four years old, used to like very much to go to church, and especially enjoyed the singing. One day, the choir sang, "Rock of ages, cleft for me," and after she got home, the little one was heard singing, very seriously, "Rock the babies, kept for me."

Easter Craft

Easter Cards
By Lina Beard and Adelia Belle Beard

Sending Easter cards is a very pretty custom, altogether too pretty to be allowed to lapse into disuse, as many customs which are merely the expression of sentiment are apt to do in this busy, practical country of ours. One experiences a great deal of pleasure in selecting from the stock of

beautiful cards found in the stores just before Easter those that seem suitable for one's friends, but more pleasure will be derived from homemade Easter cards, both to the sender and recipient; for it is true that into everything we make we put a part of ourselves, and into many a homemade article is woven loving thoughts which make the gift priceless, although the materials of which it is composed may have cost little or nothing. Several years ago the writer was visiting a friend in the country twenty miles from the nearest town where Easter cards could be purchased, but when Easter approached we sent off our cards, just the same, and I am sure our friends were as pleased with them, and more pleased, than if they had been of the most expensive kind. This is how we made them:

It was an early spring, and the woods were filled with wild-flowers, anemones and violets mostly; these we gathered, and arranging them in small bunches, stuck the stems through little slits cut in half sheets of cardstock. Underneath the bouquet we wrote the name of the person for whom it was intended, with some friendly message appropriate to the season, and signed our names. Artificial flowers may also be used if fresh ones are not available (pictured above).

To those who can paint their Easter cards we have no suggestions to offer, for they have an unlimited supply of designs at their command, and with their power of decoration, may turn almost anything into an Easter card, from a piece of satin ribbon, upon which they sketchily paint a spray of flowers, to an elaborate picture.

"Stepping through the White House" this card is called, and it represents a little chicken breaking through its shell (pictured in the middle of the above photo). The pattern of the chicken is given in the diagrams. Fig. 1, the head and neck,

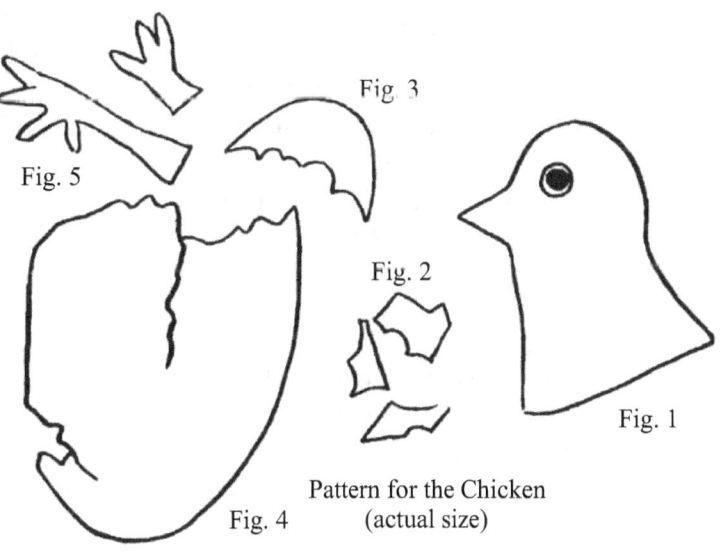

Pattern for the Chicken (actual size)

are cut from yellow paper; Figs. 2, 3, and 4, the main part and fragments of shell, are of white paper, and Fig. 5, the feet, of black paper. These are glued to cardstock, as shown in the photo on the previous page. The eye and bill are made black with a pen or marker.

Another idea! Use a computer program to create unique cards for your friends and family. There are lots of different programs available and most computers come with at least one program. You might include scriptures in the cards, or perhaps you could write your own poem! ~Amy

Luther's Easter Hymn

In the bonds of Death He lay
Who for our offence was slain;
But the Lord is risen today,
Christ hath brought us life again.
Wherefore let us all rejoice,
Singing loud with cheerful voice.
Hallelujah!

Of the sons of men, was none
Who could break the bonds of Death;
Sin this mischief dire had done;
Innocent was none on earth,
Wherefore Death grew strong and bold,
Would all men in his prison hold.
Hallelujah!

Jesus Christ, God's only Son,
Came at last our foe to smite,
All our sins away hath done,
Done away Death's power and might.
Only the form of Death is left,
Of his sting he is bereft,
Hallelujah!

That was a wondrous war, I trow,
When Life and Death together fought,
But Life hath triumph'd o'er his foe,
Death is mock'd and set at naught.
'Tis even as the Scripture saith,
Christ through death has conquer'd Death;
Hallelujah!

The rightful Paschal Lamb is He,
On whom alone we all must live,
Who to death upon the tree,
Himself in wondrous love did give.
Faith strikes His blood upon the door.
Death fell, and dares not harm us more.
Hallelujah!

Let us keep high festival
On this most blessed day of days,
When God his mercy showed to all;
Our Sun is risen with brightest rays,
And our dark hearts rejoice to see
Sin and night before Him flee.
Hallelujah!

To the supper of the Lord,
Gladly will we come today;
The word of peace is now restored,
The old leaven is put away.
Christ will be our food alone.
Faith no life but His doth own.
Hallelujah!

Tuesday Before Palm Sunday

Easter Eggs, Part 1
By Christoph Von Schmid

Many centuries ago there dwelt in a little valley surrounded by mountains a few poor charcoal-burners. The narrow valley was closed in on every side by trees and rocks. The huts of the poor peasants lay scattered around. A few cherry or plum trees planted beside each hut—a little tillage and pasture land—a patch of flax and hemp—a cow and one or two goats, constituted all their riches, though they earned a trifle besides by burning charcoal for the iron works in the mountains. Poor as they were, however, they were nevertheless a very happy little community, for they wanted nothing else. Their hardy mode of life, their constant toil and temperate habits, made them very healthy; and in these poor little huts you might see (what you would seek in vain in palaces) men over a hundred years of age.

One day, when the corn was just beginning to ripen, and the heat had become very great in the mountains, a little charcoal-girl, who had been tending her goats, came running down, out of breath, to tell her parents that some strange people had arrived in the valley, who wore wonderful clothes and spoke with a strange accent—a beautiful lady with two children and a very old man, who, though he also wore a very rich dress, seemed to be her servant.

"Ah," said the little girl, "the poor people are hungry and thirsty and very tired. I met them in the mountains, as I was searching for a stray goat, and I showed them the way to our valley. We must take them out something to eat and drink, and see whether, among the neighbors and ourselves, we cannot get them lodgings for the night."

Her parents immediately got some oaten bread, milk, and goat's cheese, and hastened out to meet them. The strangers, meanwhile, had been resting themselves under the cool shade of the bushes—the lady was sitting upon a moss-grown stone, and had drawn a white veil over her face. One of the children, a very pretty delicate little girl, sat upon her knee; the old servant, a man of venerable appearance, was employed in unloading the mule which they had with them; and the other child, a handsome, lively boy, was giving a handful of thistles to the mule, who ate them contentedly.

The charcoal-burner and his wife approached the strange lady with deference, for her graceful figure, noble bearing, and flowing white dress proclaimed her to be of high rank.

"Just look," said the charcoal-burner's wife, in a low tone, to her husband, "at the beautiful pointed collar, and the lace cuffs which just show her delicate hands; and her shoes are as white as cherry blossoms, and spangled with silver flowers!"

"Hold your tongue," said her husband, "you are always thinking of some nonsense like that. Great folk are entitled to fine clothes; but after all, dress does not make a person one whit better, and the poor lady, in spite of her beautiful shoes, has had to walk many a weary step over the rough roads!"

They advanced and offered their bread, milk, and cheese to the strange lady. She threw back her veil, and they were both filled with admiration of her beauty and the gentle expression of her features. She thanked them very much, and immediately gave a cup of the milk to the child in her lap: and the tears streamed down her cheeks, as the poor little thing clutched the cup fast with both her hands and drank eagerly. The pretty boy, too, came and drank. She then gave them some bread, and afterwards drank herself and ate some of the bread; while the strange man cut huge slices of the cheese, and seemed to enjoy it very much. Meanwhile the cottagers, young and old, came out of their huts, and stood round, in a circle watching the newcomers with curious and wondering eyes.

As soon as the old man had done eating, he earnestly begged them to provide, in some of their huts, a little room for the lady for a short time, promising that she should not be a burden to them, but should pay liberally for everything.

"Ah, yes," said the lady herself, in a soft, pleasing voice, "do take pity on an unhappy mother and her two little ones, whom fate has driven from their home!"

The men went together to consult in what house she could most conveniently be received. In the upper part of the valley there was a little stream which burst out from among the red marble cliffs, and fell from rock to rock in a mass of milky foam, turning in its course a mill which hung upon the edge of the precipice. On the opposite side of the stream the miller had built another pretty little house. Like all the other houses in the valley, it was but a wooden one; but it was extremely pretty, charmingly shaded by overhanging cherry trees and surrounded by a garden. This house the miller offered the strange lady to take her abode in.

"My new cottage, above yonder," said he, pointing with his hand, "I most cheerfully give up to you, just as it stands. It is perfectly new; no one has ever lived in it yet. I built it as a place to which I might retire when I should give up the mill to my son. It was only yesterday it was completed, and today you can take possession of it, just as if I had built it expressly for yourself. I am sure you will like it."

The good lady was delighted with this friendly offer, and after she had rested a little, went to look at the cottage. She carried the little girl in her arms, and the old man led the boy by the hand, while the miller took charge of the mule. To the great joy of the miller, she was delighted with the little house. It was already provided with a table, and a few chairs and bedsteads.

The lady had brought on the mule's back some handsome carpets and covers; so she was able to take up her lodging for the night, thanking God that, after their long wanderings, He had brought them to so pleasant a spot.

Very early next morning the lady and her two children came out of their cottage, to take a look at the surrounding country, for the day before they were too tired to do so. She was charmed with the prospect. The huts of the charcoal-burners lay far below, as if sown in twos or threes in the green valley. The mill-stream wound, clear as silver, midway between on the hills and cliffs, which were covered with green brushwood on which the goats were browsing, and it presented, in the morning sunshine, a picture which no art could surpass....

Summer and autumn passed, and the winter came. In this wild region it was very severe. For months together the little huts in the valley lay as if buried in snow, the smoking chimneys and parts of the roofs alone appearing above the white covering. Not a bit of the space between the rocks could be seen, the mill stood still, and the waterfalls hung stiff and noiseless upon the cliffs. Neighbors seldom could meet each other now; and when at last the snow disappeared, and the spring returned once more, great was the delight of all.

The children of the valley immediately came up to the mill and brought to the two little strangers, Edmund and Blanda, the earliest violets and cowslips which they could find in the valley; and as soon as there were sufficient of these sweet spring flowers, they made for them a most beautiful blue and yellow garland.

"I must make some return to these kind children also," said the lady. "I shall get up a little festival for them next Easter Day; for it is right to make these holidays as happy as possible to children. But what shall I give them? At Christmas I was able to give them apples and nuts which I sent for the purpose; but at this season one has nothing in the house but a few eggs. Nature has not yet produced her rich stores. The trees and bushes are without fruits or berries—eggs are the earliest gift of the spring."

"Ah, yes!" said Martha, "if the eggs were not so much all of one color. White is certainly a nice color, but the various tints of the fruits and berries, and the rosy cheeks of the apples are far prettier."

"Your suggestion is not a bad one," said her kind mistress; "I will boil the eggs hard, and color them in the boiling, which can be easily done. The children, I am sure, will be highly delighted with the different colors."

The clever lady knew all about the different roots and mosses which may be used for dyeing: and she colored the eggs in a variety of ways; some she made blue, others yellow, others a beautiful rose color; and some she wrapped in tender green leaves, which left their pattern on the eggs, and gave them an extremely pretty variegated appearance. On some of them she wrote a little rhyme.

"Yes," said the miller, when he saw them, "these colored eggs are just the thing for the festival—now that Nature has laid aside her white attire, and dresses herself out in all her varied hues. The good lady does just like God, who not only gives His fruits an agreeable flavor, but also makes them beautiful and pleasing to the eye—as He dyes the cherry red, the plum purple, and the pear yellow, so does she dye her eggs."

The lady now sent Martha round the valley to invite all the children who were of the same age as Edmund and Blanda to a little juvenile festival on Easter Day.

Easter Day, this season, proved an extremely beautiful spring day—a true resurrection of nature. The sun seemed so lovely and warm, the sky so clear and blue, that it was really charming and imparted new life to everything around. The meadows in the valley were already a lovely green, and here and there dotted with flowers. Every one enjoyed the sight of enjoyment and happiness.

Long before daybreak the lady and old Kuno were upon their way to the church, which lay at a distance of more than two miles beyond the mountains, Edmund and Blanda remaining at home meanwhile, under Martha's care; and the grown-up people of the valley, with the elder children who were equal to the journey, accompanied her to church. Towards midday the lady reached home, riding on the mule which Kuno led, but it was long after this hour, in fact nearly evening, when the cottagers and their children returned.

The moment the lady returned, her little guests, who had been left home, and were anxiously longing for her return, came up full of joy, all dressed out in their little finery, and assembled before her door. She came out with Edmund and Blanda, greeted them all affectionately, and brought them into the garden, which Kuno had taken great pains in improving last year, and had extended to the foot of the precipice. The lady sat down on a little bench under a tree, and called the children close to her. They all thronged around, and looked up to her with affectionate smiles while she told them in simple language the beautiful old story of the first Easter Day.

The children all listened to her with great attention, and when she had finished she paused for a moment and looked round at her young hearers. Among them she noticed a brother and sister dressed in deep mourning, and, hearing that they had lost their mother a few days before, she showed them how they might draw comfort from the story of the resurrection, and look forward in joyous hope to beholding their dear mother once more in Paradise.

She now brought the children to the shelter of the rock, where Kuno had prepared a large oval table upon a nice graveled spot. The table was covered with a colored cloth, and seats of fresh green sods were arranged around it. The children, with Edmund and Blanda in the midst of them, took their places at it. All eyes beamed with joy, and with anticipation of the coming entertainment, and it would not be easy to imagine a more interesting sight than the little circle of yellow and brown locks and happy faces which surrounded the table. "A wreath of the most beautiful lilies and roses," said the lady to herself, "is nothing in comparison with it!"

A large earthen dish filled with warm custard was now placed upon the table, and before each of the little guests was set a nice new bowl, filled with the custard. They enjoyed it exceedingly. The lady then brought them out through a side gate of the garden, into the little pine grove which stood close by. There were nice green plots of grass between the young trees, and here the lady told each of the children to make a little nest with the moss which grew in profusion upon the rocks and trees round about. They joyfully obeyed, those who were not able to make the nest themselves being helped by their more clever companions; and then they all carefully marked their own nests.

Then she brought them again into the garden; when, behold! They found upon the table a huge cake—made with eggs, and shaped like an immense crown. Each of the children was helped to a large slice, and while they were eating, Martha slipped quietly into the grove with a large basketful of colored eggs, and laid them in the little nests. The blue, red, yellow, or variegated eggs looked very pretty amongst the delicate green moss, of which the nests were formed.

When the children had finished eating, the lady called them to come and look at their nests—and, behold! In every nest were found five eggs of the same color, with a verse upon one of the number.... They all consisted of but a few simple and unstudied words; they were inscribed both on the eggs which she had already distributed, and on another set which she afterwards divided among the children. Some of them were as follows:

*To thee our earthly food we owe,
Grant us, O Lord, thy gifts to know!*

*One thing is needful—only one—
Love God, my child, and Him alone.*

*On God's protecting arm rely;
To Him in all thy sorrows fly!*

*A docile child its parents' will
Is ever ready to fulfill.*

*The liar's steps shame will pursue;
His word is doubted, e'en when true.*

*A truly good and pious man
Assists his neighbor when he can.*

*Gentle thoughts and self-control
Bring peace and comfort to the soul.*

*The world and all its joys decay;
Virtue alone endures for aye.*

The spring and summer passed over in the valley without anything remarkable happening. The charcoal-burners tilled their little farms, and then went to the forest to burn charcoal; their wives attended to the housekeeping at home, and reared a great number of hens; and the children would often ask whether Easter would not soon come again. But the noble lady was often very unhappy. Her faithful old servant, who till now had always been at her side, and who in the commencement used to make journeys of greater or less extent for her upon her business, was no longer able to leave the valley, for his health began to fail; and, indeed, when autumn came, and the leaves began to grow brown upon the bushes, he could hardly even leave the house to enjoy what he dearly loved, a little bask in the genial sunshine. His mistress shed many an anxious tear for the good old man who was her last support, and she bitterly felt getting no news from her dear native land, and being shut out from the rest of the world in this secluded valley.

To be continued!

Easter Cooking

Matzo Bread By Amy Puetz

This unleavened bread is the kind used by the Jews during the Passover. A bread similar to this is what Jesus broke and gave to His disciples at the last supper. Read Exodus 12:8 and Deuteronomy 16:1-8 to see why the Israelites ate unleavened bread during the Passover. Sometimes the Passover meal is also called the Feast of Unleavened Bread.

1 cup flour
½ cup water
½ tsp. salt (optional)

Preheat oven to 450° F. Cover a cookie sheet with parchment paper. If using salt, mix it and the flour together and add water. Otherwise combine water and flour together. Use extra flour to knead the dough for a minute or two. Break the dough into egg sized pieces and roll out very thin. Put the bread on the parchment paper (picture at top). Poke all over with a fork to keep it from bubbling up in the middle. Bake for 10 to 12 minutes. Check at 5 to 7 minutes to insure it is not getting overdone.

May be made using wheat flour (white or whole), rye, barley, spelt, or oat.

Above - matzo bread before and after baking.

Left - To give as a gift, wrap in plastic wrap or pretty paper and tie with a ribbon.

Wednesday Before Palm Sunday

Easter Eggs, Part 2
By Christoph Von Schmid

A circumstance occurred, too, which filled the good lady with no little alarm. One morning some of the charcoal-burners came home from the forest and told the miller that the night before, as they were sitting quietly by their burning heap, four strange men suddenly came upon them, with iron helmets, and coats of mail, and with huge swords by their side, and long lances in their hands. They said they were retainers of the Count von Schroffeneck, who had come into the mountains with a large train; and they inquired about everything in the neighborhood. The miller hastened with his news to the lady, who at that moment was sitting by Kuno's sick-bed. The moment he mentioned the name of Schroffeneck, she turned pale and cried out: "Oh my God! It is my deadliest foe—I am sure he seeks nothing else but my life. I hope the people did not let the strangers know where I am living!" The miller assured her that as far as he knew they had not mentioned her at all.

"The men," said he, "only warmed themselves at the fire, and went away before daybreak; but they are still, no doubt, reconnoitering through the mountains."

"Dear Oswald!" said the lady to the miller, "ever since I came to your house, I have always found you a conscientious, upright, honest man. I will, therefore, tell you my whole history, and the anxiety which now fills my heart, for I reckon upon your counsel and assistance.

"I am Rosalind, daughter of the Duke of Burgundy. Two noble lords, Hanno of Schroffeneck, and Arno of Lindenburg, were suitors for my hand. Hanno was the richest and most powerful lord in the country around, and had the largest train of retainers, and the strongest castles; but he was wanting in virtue and nobleness of soul. Arno was the bravest and noblest knight in the land; but, in comparison with his rival, he was poor, for he had inherited from his generous father nothing but one old castle and had never attempted to enlarge his possessions by violence. To him, notwithstanding, I gave my hand with my father's consent, and I brought him large domains, and many strong castles as my dowry. Our life was a paradise on earth.

"But Hanno of Schroffeneck conceived a deadly hate against me and my husband, and became our mortal enemy, though he concealed his hatred, and made no open display of it for a time. At last my husband was called to accompany the emperor in his expedition against the Muslims. Hanno was summoned also; but he contrived, under various pretexts, to delay his preparations, merely promising to join the army as soon as possible. But while my husband and his vassals were engaged in the most distant part of the kingdom, fighting for their country, the false Hanno invaded our territory, and there was not a soul to oppose him. He laid everything waste far and wide, and stormed one castle after another, till at last nothing remained for me but to fly secretly with my two darling children. My good old Kuno was my only guardian angel upon this perilous flight during which I was constantly exposed to Hanno's pursuit. He brought me to these mountains, where I have lived so peacefully in this secluded and unknown valley. Here it was my purpose to remain till my husband should return from the war, and recover our domains from the usurper. Kuno used to go from time to time to the great world, to learn news of the war, but he always came back with sad tidings; the wicked Hanno was still in possession of our lands, and the war was still continuing with varying success at the frontier. But now for nearly a year my good Kuno has been sick, and all this time I know nothing either of my country or my beloved husband. Alas! Perhaps he has long fallen under the sword of the enemy. Perhaps Hanno, who is now so close to us, has discovered my secret hiding-place—and if so, what will become of me? Oh! Beg the charcoal-burners, dear Oswald, not to betray me!"

"What, betray you?" cried the miller, "I will answer for them all—every one of them would die for you! Before the hateful tyrant of Schroffeneck shall lay a finger upon you, he will first have to kill us all. Do not be afraid, noble lady!"

The charcoal-burners repeated the same protestations when the miller spoke to them. "Just let him come!" they cried, "We will give him a lesson with our bill-hooks!"

Meanwhile the good lady's days were spent in fear and anxiety. She would hardly venture out of the house, and never let her children from the doors. Her life was very anxious and sad. But when all was quiet again in the mountain, and nothing more was heard of the armed men, she at last ventured to take a walk. It was a lovely day, late in the harvest, after a long continuance of rain. A few hundred paces from her hut stood a sort of rustic chapel, built of rough pine boards, and open in front. But it contained a very pretty picture of the Flight into Egypt, which Kuno had once brought home on one of his journeys, to cheer the good lady in her exile.

Behind the chapel rose a steep wall of rock, and in front stood a few pine trees, which formed a pleasant shade over the entrance. The place had such an air of quiet and repose, that one felt a pleasure in staying there. A grassy path between picturesque rocks and shrubs led to it, and it was the lady's favorite walk. This time, however, she was not entirely without anxiety. She knelt down for a while with her children at the little stool at the entrance of the chapel. She prayed for a while, and then sat down upon the bench. The children meanwhile were gathering blackberries and amusing themselves by comparing them to little black bunches of grapes, till by degrees they had strayed some distance away.

While the lady sat thus alone, suddenly a pilgrim appeared among the rocks and approached the chapel. He wore a long black dress, and a short cloak over it. His hat was adorned with scallop-shells, and in his hand he carried a long white staff. He appeared to be very old, but was still a stately, handsome man: his long white hair, which flowed down upon his shoulders, and his beard, were as white as snow, but his cheeks still retained all the bloom of the rose. The lady was alarmed when she saw the stranger. He saluted her respectfully and addressed her, but she was very cautious and reserved in her conversation, and looked with great coldness upon him, as though she wished to discover whether she ought to trust a total stranger, of whom she knew absolutely nothing.

"Noble lady," said the pilgrim at last, "be not afraid of me, I am not such a stranger as you think. You are Rosalind of Burgundy. I am well acquainted with the cruel destiny which drove you to take refuge amid these rugged rocks. Your husband, too, from whom you are near three years parted, is well known to me. While you have been living in this distant spot many changes have taken place in the world. If you are anxious to hear about the good Arno of Lindenburg, and if his memory still lives in your heart, I can give you some good news about him. The war is over. The Christian army is coming home, crowned with the laurels of victory. Your husband has recovered the places that were wrested from him. The wicked Hanno escaped into the fastnesses of this mountain; but even from this last retreat he must soon be driven. The sole, the ardent wish of your husband is to find once more his beloved spouse."

"Oh God! What joyful news!" exclaimed the lady as she sank on her knees, while big tears rolled down her cheeks. "From my heart I thank Thee, Oh God," she said. "Thou hast seen my tears, Thou hast heard my silent sighs, Thou hast granted my ceaseless prayers. Oh! Arno, Arno, may that happy moment soon come, when I shall see you once more, and present to you those children who were babies when you left us, and who now for the first time can call you by the endearing name of father!"

"Oh stranger!" said she to the pilgrim, "who can doubt whether I still cherish my husband's memory, and have his love still fresh and ardent in my heart? My children, come here," said she, turning to her two little ones, who stood at a distance watching the strange man with curiosity, but too shy to approach.

"Edmund," said she, addressing the boy, and telling him at the same time not to be afraid, "Edmund, repeat for this stranger the little prayer we say every morning for your father." The boy, clasping his hands devoutly, and raising his eyes to heaven, as in actual prayer, repeated in a loud, impressive, and affecting tone, the following words: "Dear heavenly Father, look down on us two poor little orphans! Our father is in the wars—oh! Save him from death. We resolve to be good, that we may give joy to our dear father when he comes back to us. Oh! Hear our prayer."

"And you, Blanda," said she to a little yellow-haired, rosy-cheeked girl, "repeat the prayer we say every evening for your father, before we retire to rest."

"Dear heavenly Father, before we retire to rest, we pray to Thee for our father. May he sleep in peace this night, and be guarded from all harm by Thy holy angels. Send down sweet sleep to our mother, that she may forget her great griefs for a while; or, should soft sleep be not granted her, let it fall on the eyelids of our dear father. May that happy morn soon dawn which shall behold us united once more!"

"Amen, Amen," said the mother, clasping her hands, and looking tearfully to heaven.

At this moment the pilgrim burst into tears and wept aloud. He flung off the pilgrim's garb, hair, mantle, and frock, and stood before them in the dazzling uniform of a knight, glittering with gold and purple. He was in the full glow of youthful beauty, full of health and vigor. He stretched out his arms towards his wife and children, and in a voice of the most heartfelt emotion, exclaimed, "Oh! Rosalind, my wife, and Edmund and Blanda, my dear children!"

This sudden, unexpected joy almost overpowered the wife. The children, who, when they had seen the pilgrim weeping, looked at their mother as if to beg her to help him, were now, when they heard their own names, startled, and almost frightened at what they believed was a miracle occurring before their eyes; for they imagined nothing less than that, as their mother had often told them in the legends she used to relate to them, the old man changed himself into a beautiful youth—or an angel from heaven; so much were they struck by the appearance of their father, who in reality was the handsomest knight in the whole Christian army.

What was their delight when their mother assured them, that the handsome gentleman was their beloved father, of whom she had so often told them; and in this happy meeting the hours fled away almost as rapidly as though they had been moments.

Rosalind learned from her husband's conversation that he had been coming in all haste, with strong escort, to convey her from this retreat; but that the steepness of the roads had compelled him to leave his train behind, and to hasten forward alone, on foot, in this pilgrim garb, which he had often used before, in order to see her the sooner, to satisfy himself by personal inspection that she and her children were well, and to prepare her for the joyful news. She now asked how he had discovered her retreat.

"Dearest Rosalind," said he, "this happy reunion is the fruit of your own charity to the poor, especially to the poor children of this valley. Had it not been for your kind heart, we should not have met so soon—perhaps we should never have met again, for you were beset on all sides by our enemies, and might easily have fallen into their hands. It was not till the arrival of my party in the mountains that Hanno finally retreated."

He showed her the painted egg with the inscription:

On God's protecting arm rely; To Him in all thy sorrows fly!

"This egg," said he, "was, under God, the means of reuniting us. For a long time I had been sending numberless messengers in search of you, but always without success. At last Eckbert, one of my squires, whom I had given up for lost, he had been so long absent, returned from an expedition. He had fallen into a ravine, and was on the point of perishing with hunger, when a strange youth saved his life by giving him a couple of eggs to eat, and gave him this egg also, with the beautiful inscription, as a souvenir of his escape. Eckbert showed me the egg, and what was my surprise, when at the first glance I discovered your handwriting! We instantly set out, and rode to the great marble works in which the good youth was employed, and he directed me hither. Had not your kind heart prompted you to give this little feast of eggs to the children—had not your goodness inspired you to think of the wants of the soul as well as of the body, and to write these pretty rhymes upon the eggs—had not you all, you, my dear little Edmund, and my darling Blanda, been so kind to the strange youth, we might never have enjoyed this happy day! I shall have this egg, therefore, cased in gold and pearls, and hung up in our castle chapel as an everlasting memorial of the event."

Meanwhile, evening had begun to close, and the stars began to appear here and there in the clear heaven. Count Arno with his lady leaning upon his arm, and the children tripping before them, came to their humble dwelling. Here new joys awaited them. The squire and his deliverer, Fridolin, were already there, and had told the news to Kuno, whom the joyous tidings of his master's return had made almost well again. The good youth, Fridolin, first advanced and saluted the lady and her children most joyfully, as old acquaintances. Next came Eckbert, the squire, who owed his life to the eggs. "Permit me, dear countess," said he, approaching respectfully, "to kiss the hand to which, under God's guidance, I am indebted for my life!"

The count embraced Kuno as his most trusty servant, and shook with true gratitude the hand of the honest miller, who stood by in full holiday costume in his blue Sunday coat. They all supped in happiness and contentment.

The next morning the valley was a scene of joyous excitement. The news of the arrival of the lady's husband, a great, very great lord, set them all in commotion. Big and little came up to see him; and the little hut was surrounded by the people. The count, with his wife and children, came out and received them all affectionately, thanking them all for their kindness to his wife and little ones. "Oh, we are not her benefactors," they replied, with tears in their eyes, "'tis she, 'tis she, who is our greatest benefactress!" The count talked with them for a long time, speaking individually to each, and left them all impressed by his kindness.

Meanwhile the count's train had, with the assistance of some charcoal-burners, discovered a road into the valley. Several knights, and a host of retainers on horseback and on foot, marched, amid the sound of trumpets, between two wooded mountains into the valley, their helmets and lances glittering in the sunbeams. They saluted their long-lost mistress with heart-felt joy, and their shouts of triumph were reechoed by the rocks all around.

Count Arno remained for a few days, and the evening before his departure, with his wife and children and Kuno and the rest of his train, he entertained all the inhabitants of the valley at a feast. The table presented a very motley appearance with the miller and charcoal-burners scattered amid knights and men-at-arms. At the close, he distributed rich presents among his guests, especially to the worthy miller; Martha remained in the countess's service. He provided especially for the mother, brother, and sister of the good youth Fridolin.

"For you, my dear little friends," said he to the children, "I shall establish an annual festival in memory of my wife's stay among such good people. Every Easter, eggs, of all varieties of color, shall be distributed among the children."

"And I," said the countess, "will extend this custom throughout our entire dominions, and order that colored eggs shall be similarly distributed there, in memory of my deliverance." And she kept her word: and the eggs were called Easter Eggs; and this pretty custom, by degrees, extended throughout the entire country.

EASTER HYMN

Christ the Lord is risen today,
Sons of men and angels say:
Raise your joys and triumphs high,
Sing, ye heavens, and earth reply.

Love's redeeming work is done,
Fought the fight, the battle won:
Lo! our Sun's eclipse is o'er;
Lo! He sets in blood no more.

Vain the stone, the watch, the seal;
Christ hath burst the gates of hell!
Death in vain forbids His rise;
Christ hath opened Paradise!

Lives again our glorious King:
Where, O Death, is now thy sting?
Once He died, our souls to save:
Where thy victory, O Grave?

BY CHARLES WESLEY

Easter Quiz

The Easter Story By Amy Puetz

See how much you know about the Easter story. Match the answers on the right with the questions on the left. Answers are below.

A) How many times did Peter disown Jesus?

B) This man asked for Jesus' body.

C) Jesus gave this man the responsibility of taking care of his mother.

D) According to the gospel of John, what woman went to the tomb?

E) Who betrayed Jesus?

F) Who was the high priest at the time of Jesus death?

G) In the gospel of Matthew, what color was the cloak that the Romans mockingly put on Jesus?

H) Who was the father-in-law of the high priest?

I) How much did the high priest pay Judas to betray Jesus?

J) According to the gospel of John, what was Jesus last statement on the cross?

1) John

2) Caiaphas

3) Annas

4) Three

5) Mary Magdalene

6) Scarlet

7) "It is finished"

8) Judas

9) Joseph of Arimathea

10) Thirty silver coins

Answers: A-4, B-9, C-1, D-5, E-8, F-2, G-6, H-3, I-10, J-7

Thursday Before Palm Sunday

Playmates in Egypt
By Elma Ehrlich Levinger

Every day, when the sun was high in the heavens, little Rachel trudged through the hot sands which scorched her bare brown feet, a loaf of black bread in her basket and a cruse of water upon her shoulder. Thus she and many other young children of the house of Israel brought food and drink to their fathers and mothers and older brothers, who toiled from sunrise until far into the night in the brick-yards of Pharaoh, ruler of Egypt. One day it happened that Rachel was somewhat delayed in bringing the noonday meal to her parents and brother, and she made what haste she could, hurrying beneath the burning sun. But her foot slipped, and she fell, breaking her earthen cruse upon the road and spilling the water, that was in it, upon the ground. Then Rachel sat down by the wayside and wept bitterly; for she knew that before she could fetch more water and return with it to her parents, they would be back at their task, and, fearing the whip of the overseer, would not dare to bid her approach them, no matter how sorely they might suffer from thirst.

While she sat thus weeping, she heard a kindly voice asking: "Why grievest thou, maiden?" Looking up, she saw a youth of her own years standing beside her. He was slim and graceful, and carried himself proudly, while the golden girdle about his cool white garments and the jeweled band in his hair proclaimed him of some princely house. And Rachel drew back in fear, for she had been taught to dread every son of Egypt.

"Be not frightened, girl," said the youth, speaking softly, "for I will do thee no harm. Tell me why thou weepest, and I will seek to bring thee comfort, for no one has ever asked succor in vain of Pethis son of Randor."

Rachel was now more frightened than before, for Randor was chief of the taskmasters in the brick-yards of Pharaoh, and the children of Israel had often suffered through his hardness of heart. She would have run away from his son, but the boy detained her, and spoke comforting words to her, until her fear and terror had gone. Then she told him of the misfortune that had befallen her, and wept anew as she pointed to the broken cruse; for she grieved that her poor mother must toil all day without a drop of water to slake her burning thirst.

But Pethis laughed a little, and drew a flask from his girdle and gave it to her; and, fearing that she would come too late to her parents, he himself sought out their taskmaster, and bade him allow little Rachel to go to them. The man obeyed, though sullenly, for he knew that Randor, the father of the youth, was a mighty man in Egypt.

This was but the beginning of the friendship between the princely boy of Egypt and the little daughter of the Hebrew slaves. Often, as Rachel passed down the road at noon, after bringing food and drink to the brick-yards, Pethis would start from the bushes by the roadside and greet her and bid her linger a while, that they might play together. For the lad had no brothers and sisters of his own, and was often very lonely for a playmate.

First he would spread out a feast for her upon the rocks—wheaten bread and dates and sweet wine—and she would eat and drink and be satisfied, often wishing that she might save some of the dainty food for her mother, but trembling lest anyone might come to know of her friendship with the Egyptian prince. Then, screened by the shrubs—for the lad, too, feared lest word should come to his father that he spent many hours with a daughter of the Hebrews—the two would toss his golden ball, one to the other, or run races, which Rachel would never fail to win, for she was as fleet of foot as the wild gazelle upon the mountains. Then, wearied with play at last, they would cast themselves down to rest by a tiny stream of water that they had discovered bubbling among the rocks. Here Rachel would weave garlands from the flowers Pethis gathered and bind them about her dark braids, as she told him the stories she had heard from her father—of Abraham's leaving his home for a strange country, of Jacob who dreamed of a ladder down which great, white-winged angels descended as he slept, and of Joseph whom his brethren had sold into Egypt as a slave. In his turn, Pethis would tell her wondrous tales of the gods of his people and the deeds of strength and valor wrought by the noble warriors of his father's house.

"I am my father's only son," he would exclaim, raising himself upon his elbow, and looking up into Rachel's face, his eyes aglow with dreams. "Someday I will take his place and stand at Pharaoh's right hand and ride in his chariot when he goes to battle. And I will become a great warrior and the most powerful man in all Egypt. And then, Rachel, I will take thee to wife, and thou wilt no longer go about in mean rags; nay, thou wilt shine like a princess in gold and in snowy garments heavy with jewels."

"But, Pethis," Rachel reminded him one day, "how couldst thou take a despised daughter of the Hebrews to wife?"

Pethis was ready with his answer. "I will gain Pharaoh's ear and beseech him to free thy people, that they may live in ease and in comfort, even as they did in the days of Joseph," he promised.

"Then I wish that thou wert already a man, Pethis," sighed Rachel, "for my people groan under many burdens, and my father says that, unless our God speedily sends us a deliverer, we must surely perish." She grieved as she spoke, never dreaming how soon that deliverer was to come.

For, before many moons, strange rumors passed among the Hebrews as they toiled in the brick-yards, and Pethis told Rachel of two strangers who had appeared before Pharaoh and demanded that he set the children of Israel free. Then an age of many wonders began for Egypt—strange plagues which made the land desolate and the people afraid, from Pharaoh upon his throne to the slave who ground the grain in the courtyard. Yet Pharaoh would not listen to the word of the God of the Hebrews, and did not permit his slave-people to depart. The land groaned in those days under new afflictions, for all growing things sickened and died; the locusts swarmed above the land of Egypt; and, at last, so terrible a darkness covered the earth, that no man from among the Egyptians dared to leave his house, but remained in terror and fear behind barred doors.

Safe within her father's hut, for there was light in the dwelling-places of the children of Israel, little Rachel sobbed in terror, for she was sore afraid; her mother wept also, but her father was strong in hope. "Fear not," he told them, "for the God of our fathers has wrought these wonders through His servant, Moses. And still greater wonders will He perform before Pharaoh will permit us to depart."

Even as he spoke, Rachel's brother rushed into the house. "Father," he cried, and his face was white with a strange terror, "it is as the man of God has said: the Lord has passed through the midst of Egypt, and the firstborn of every house of Egypt lies dead—from the firstborn of Pharaoh upon his throne unto the firstborn of the captive that is in the dungeon. For the Lord has slain the firstborn son in every household of Egypt; only the eldest of the sons of Israel has He saved."

Then the father and mother and brother of Rachel praised the God of their fathers that He had not afflicted them, and that the last of His signs and wonders had come to pass; for now they were sure that the time was at hand when He would lead them out of Egypt. But little Rachel hid her face in her mother's lap, and wept bitterly; she knew that her dear playmate, Pethis, was the firstborn of his father, and that she would never look upon his face again.

Easter Carol
By George Newell Lovejoy

O Earth! Throughout thy borders
Re-don thy fairest dress;
And everywhere, O Nature!
Throb with new happiness;
Once more to new creation
Awake, and death gainsay,
For death is swallowed up of life,
And Christ is risen today!

Let peals of jubilation
Ring out in all the lands;
With hearts of deep elation
Let sea with sea clasp hands;
Let one supreme Te Deum
Roll round the world's highway,
For death is swallowed up of life,
And Christ is risen today!

Easter Craft

Wall Hanging - History of the Passover
By Amy Puetz

You will need:
Colored cardstock or paper
Ribbon
Double sided tape and scissors

1. Copy the pictures and header on the next three pages onto colored cardstock or paper.

2. Cut out the pictures.

3. On one end of the ribbon knot a loop. This will be how the ribbon is hung. Use double sided tape to attach the pictures to the ribbon.

An Egg-speriment
To Put an Egg in a Glass Bottle
By Melville De Lancey Landon and Mark Twain

To put an egg into a bottle whose mouth is seemingly too small to receive it: take a glass bottle with a mouth about an inch and a quarter in diameter. Individual glass tea bottles work well. Into the mouth thrust a piece of burning paper. Quickly cork it with a hard boiled egg from which the shell has been removed. Use a small or normal sized egg, extra large eggs are too big! The flame exhausts the air in the bottle, and as soon as the bottle cools off, the outer atmosphere will drive the egg into the bottle. The egg will lengthen out a little on going in, but will resume its original shape as soon as it passes in.

Adult assistance required for this experiment! More information about this experiment may be found online. Just search for, "put an egg in a bottle" and several interesting links are shown. There are even a couple of videos that show it being done. ~Amy

The History of the Passover

Exodus 11 & 12
Matthew, Mark, Luke, John

The Passover is a Jewish holiday celebrating their deliverance from Egypt. God sent a plague against the firstborn in the land of Egypt but the Israelites were spared. The Lord passed over their houses because their door frames were marked with blood.

Jesus died on Passover and was the ultimate sacrifice. He died for our sins.

As a boy Jesus celebrated the Passover in Jerusalem.
Luke 2:41-50

The Triumphal Entry

Jesus Carrying His Cross

The Crucifixion

On the Third Day Jesus Rose Again Then He Returned to Heaven

Countdown to Easter

Friday Before Palm Sunday

Harold's Happy Easter
& The Wonder Egg

By Carolyn Sherwin Bailey

Harold's Happy Easter By Carolyn Sherwin Bailey

For many, many weeks Harold had been obliged to sit still in a big arm chair because he had a sprained ankle.

"I don't mind it so much now," he said to his dear mother, when it was snowing and gray clouds shut out the sunshine, "but what shall I do when the spring comes?"

"We shall see, Harold," his dear mother answered with a smile.

The spring came presently. Blue sky and yellow sunshine and red-breasted robins and white snowdrops made the spring. As Harold sat in his armchair by the window, he watched the boy who worked for the florist pass by with a huge pot of tall, white lilies.

"It will be Easter Day soon," Harold said, and a little round tear squeezed itself out of each one of his big brown eyes and trickled down his cheeks. "I wish I could keep Easter."

"Shut your eyes, Harold, until I say ready," laughed his dear mother. Harold was so surprised that he shut his eyes quickly, closing inside all the other little round tears which had been waiting to squeeze themselves out.

"Ready!" called his dear mother. Harold opened his eyes. Oh, the surprise that awaited him!

Upon the play table right in front of his big chair he saw all these treasures. There were six white eggs which Biddy Short Legs, his little brown hen, had laid for him, and five of them his dear mother had boiled. There was his box of paints of many colors. There was a pot of white paste. There were scissors and many pieces of tissue paper, pink and green and white and yellow and blue.

"Now we will make these eggs into beautiful Easter gifts for all our friends," explained Harold's dear mother.

So they made one egg into a funny doctor man's head for the kind doctor man who had taken care of Harold for so many weeks. He had a smiling face painted on the egg and big black spectacles cut from black tissue paper were pasted on. A stiff white paper collar was pasted about the smaller end of the egg and a stiff black paper hat was pasted upon the larger end of the egg. Oh, such a funny little Easter gift as it made!

Then Harold painted two beautiful eggs for the little twin girls who lived next door. First, his mother drew on each egg a picture of a white lily and Harold painted the outside of each egg around the picture of the lily a beautiful yellow. When the yellow paint was dry, Harold's dear mother tied yellow ribbon with bows about each egg. They were very pretty indeed.

Next Harold wanted to make an Easter egg for Tommy, the kind little boy who lived across the street. So he painted one egg brown like a round, brown football. When the paint was dry his dear mother drew on the egg some fine pencil lines like the leather lacing of a football. Harold painted these lines black and the egg looked like a real football. Harold knew that Tommy's eyes would shine when he saw it.

The fourth egg was to be made into an Easter gift for little Edith who lived in the house just beyond the twins. Harold's dear mother helped him to paint a sweet little girl's face on the egg. Then they pasted on yellow braids made of braided twisted yellow tissue paper and tied at the ends with bits of pale blue ribbon. Next came a little white cap made of tissue paper with a pink tissue paper rose over each ear. Last, a full ruffle of pink tissue paper was pasted to the narrow end of the egg. It looked like a dress and made the tiny egg doll stand. It was a pretty little doll and not like any to be found in a toy shop. It would make Edith very happy.

"What shall I do with this egg?" Harold asked.

"We shall give it to Granny Gray who lives in the little lane at the end of the street and who is ill nearly always," Harold's dear mother said.

So she found a tiny basket and Harold snipped and snipped bits of tissue paper—pink and green and white and yellow and blue—until there was enough to make a nest inside the basket. In the nest they laid the egg and a little package of tea and a little jar of jelly and a little pot of cheese.

"I wish—" began Harold. Then he looked at the beautiful gifts that he had made. "Why, I can keep Easter," he finished happily.

The Wonder Egg By Carolyn Sherwin Bailey

Gretchen was the little flaxen-hair girl whose mother washed the clothes as white as snow and ironed them in dainty frills and flutings. Nancy often saw Gretchen at the kitchen door with the red wagon in which she brought home the basket of washing. Such a blue-eyed, rosy-cheeked, little German lass in a frayed frock, and a coat that was patched at the elbows.

One day it was very, very cold and Gretchen's nose was blue, too, so Nancy opened the door wide.

"Come in, little girl," she called, "and sit down by the fire. You look so very cold."

So Gretchen came shyly in and sat by the kitchen fire and toasted her toes and warmed her fingers and said a shy, goodbye, when she went away.

Another day, it was very, very rainy and Gretchen's worn shoes were quite soaked with the rain when she came, bringing the clothes. But Nancy took her hand and drew her into the kitchen, where mother took off the wet shoes and dried the feet and fitted upon them a pair of Nancy's own shoes. Oh, how little Gretchen's eyes smiled as she said, "thank you," and slipped out of the door to go home.

Then there was a very beautiful sunshiny day. The trees were hung with green leaves and a robin sang in the lilac bush, the lawn was covered with a carpet of new grass and here and there a yellow dandelion shone as yellow as gold because it was Easter Day. All the house clothes were clean. That is why Nancy was so surprised to hear a very faint knock at the front door and to see little Gretchen there, dressed in a white frock that was white and neat although it had been mended in a great many places.

She held a white parcel in her hands and when she stepped inside and took off the wrappings, there was a beautiful, big, sugar egg. It was as shining as crystal, and it had a pink candy rose on the top. In one end there was a little glass window.

"It is for you, because you have been so kind to me," said little Gretchen, eagerly. "It came with my father on the great ship from Germany. He has come to take my mother and me home when the warm days come. Look through the glass," she cried eagerly, "and see what there is for your eyes, inside."

She held the sugar egg up to Nancy's eyes and Nancy looked inside. Oh, such a wonderful sight as she saw! A little white palace set in the midst of a forest of tiny green trees. A wee little lake, and a flock of silver swans and on the banks of the lake, many gaily dressed little ladies and gentlemen.

"It is a picture of my country," said Gretchen, "for you who have been so good to me," and the washwoman's little child ran home, while Nancy stood, too happy for words, with the beautiful sugar egg in her eager hands.

What is Easter? By William Tegg

Easter Day is distinguished by its peculiar name through our Saxon ancestors, who at this season of the year held a great festival in honor of the goddess Eastor, probably the Astarte of the Eastern nations. Others think it is so called from the Saxon Oster, to rise, being the day of Christ's resurrection. The French call this Festival *paques* (from the Greek word *pascha*, and Hebrew *pesech*, i.e. passover), whence we derive the word paschal, as applied to the Lamb in the Last Supper.

Easter Craft

Easter Baskets By Amy Puetz

Easter baskets have long been a lovely tradition of Easter. For today's activity we will put together and decorate our own Easter basket.

You will need:
Basket (These may be found at second hand stores and garage sales.)
Easter Grass
Ribbons
Goodies, etc.

1. Begin by tying a ribbon around the outside of the basket.

2. Fill the basket with Easter grass. If you do not have grass it is easy to make some using green construction paper. A shredder machine makes this an easy job. For my grass, I used pink, yellow, and green construction paper. To make your own grass first clean out your shredder and then cut the construction paper to 8.5 inches. Shred as many sheets as you need. Once the paper is in little strips, crumple them up in your hands to make them kinky.

3. Now comes the fun part—adding things to your basket! Most Easter baskets have eggs (plastic or hard boiled), candy, toys, and maybe even a bunny. In the Easter basket pictured above there are Easter eggs, the bookmarks from page 41, the matzo bread from page 13, and the Hot Cross Buns from page 74.

4. To make the baskets really special include a personalized card (page 6) and a small bouquet of artificial flowers.

Themed Easter Basket Ideas

Children Basket
Coloring Book
Crayons
Stuffed animal (bunny, chick, etc.)
Candy

Adult Basket
Movies
Microwave Popcorn

Healthy Basket
Apples
Oranges
Nuts

Chocolate Basket
Chocolate Eggs
Chocolate Bunny
Chocolate Anything!

Homemade Goodies Basket
Cookies
Jam or preserves
Cup cakes
Hot Cross Buns

Saturday Before Palm Sunday

Love Triumphant
By Florence Morse Kingsley
From Tor, A Street Boy of Jerusalem, Chapter 11

To Pilate, governor of Jerusalem, seated upon the ivory chair of office before the palace, came the message from his wife. He glanced down at it with some impatience, when Diomed thrust the tablets into his hand with a hurried word of explanation.

"Have thou nothing to do with that righteous man," he read, "for I have suffered many things this day in a dream because of him."

The message was signed and sealed with the signet of the Roman princess. Pilate's pallid and heavy face whitened to the lifeless hues of the wax upon which the fateful words were written. Before him stood the drooping but still majestic figure of the Nazarene, robed in the scarlet robe of his torture and wearing the crown of thorns, a piteous sight, before which angels were veiling their shamed faces. Beyond the strong barrier of the Roman guard surged the wildest, cruelest mob of all the ages.

The governor rose to his feet slowly, and, advancing to the side of the prisoner, exclaimed in his loud, passionless voice, "Behold the man!"

Mocking laughter, furious incoherent shouts, coupled with the dreadful, insistent, "Crucify him! Crucify him!" burst out in wilder clamor.

Pilate looked forth over the sea of terrible upturned eyes, and his huge limbs trembled beneath him. Again he glanced at the pale, melancholy face of the prisoner. "The fellow is naught but a Jewish peasant," he assured himself. "And after all, what use to cast Roman justice before dogs. They will have none of it." Loudly he called for water in a basin, and in sight of them all washed his hands with spectacular solemnity, saying, "I am innocent of the blood of this just person: see ye to it!"

Back came the mocking, inhuman cry, "His blood be upon us and upon our children!"

Pilate ground his teeth in impotent rage, and, seizing Jesus roughly by the shoulder, he thrust him forward in the face of the mob. "Shall I crucify your King?" he shouted derisively.

"We have no king but Caesar!" was the blasphemous answer. And with that word was the scroll rolled up and sealed with the seven seals of wrath against the day of wrath.

And they took Jesus and led him away.

On that same day Tor was again a prisoner. The wife of Pilate in real pity had commanded that the child should be comfortably entertained in the servants' quarters until all should be over.

Diomed, to whom the carrying out of this commission was entrusted, spoke softly to the beggar in the presence of his mistress, bidding him follow. Out of sight of the lady the Greek laughed aloud in his scorn. "Here is a guest for our honorable entertainment," he said to the chief butler. "My lady the princess hath commanded it. In which of the chambers of state shall I lodge my lord?" The official sniffed his disdain. "Is it an animal?" he demanded.

"It is an animal, most sapient Clodius," laughed Diomed. "A Jewish swine—eh?—albeit a small one. Give him food and wine, excellent Clodius, for he is chiefly bone—this animal."

Tor ate, for he was starving; also he slept fitfully, for he was exhausted with fear and weeping. The sun shone warm and friendly from the cloudless spring heavens, and the child, lying upon a rug which one of the slaves had flung down for him, drowsily watched the ceaseless dance of young grape leaves in the soft warm wind.

The tumult without had suddenly ceased, and an ominous silence lay heavily upon the city. Tor thought lovingly of his Master in the intervals between dreams. "He has gone away safely with the men," he told himself. "I shall again find him, and he will heal blind folk as before." So drowsing and murmuring soft prayers to his invisible Father, the beggar child rested in the house of Pilate, while without the walls of the city his Master, the King, was already hanging upon the cross.

Within the great kitchens of the palace cooks were busy preparing the noonday meal; dishes and cups clattered cheerfully, and the merry voices of maidens burnishing the great wine-flagons mingled with the chirp and whir of sparrows flitting back and forth in the blue air.

Suddenly, and without warning, the bright light of the spring noon began to fail. There was no fog, no storm, but a veil of lurid darkness was drawn heavily across the sky. Doors and windows were thrown wide, and terror-stricken faces stared up into the threatening heavens.

Marcus, the crusty porter of the palace, stood fast in his place, his dull face blanched and terrified in the failing light. "'Tis the vengeance of the gods," he muttered. "The Man of Nazareth was innocent!"

Servants and underlings crowded the passages in terrified groups. "Open to us, Marcus," they cried, beating upon the doors till they trembled upon their heavy hinges. "Earthquake!" wailed a voice from without. "The gods are shaking this evil city!"

The porter drew the great bolts with tremulous haste, and with one accord all rushed into the street.

Scarcely knowing how it had befallen, the beggar child found himself on the street with the others, running—running he knew not whither, through empty streets which echoed his light footfalls as in the dead of night.

Somewhere, afar off, there was the tumult of a great multitude. Tor stopped to listen, then ran on, thinking of his Master, who was waiting for him in the fast-gathering darkness.

He reached a gate—which gate he knew not, but it yawned wide and unguarded. Not far away Tor could hear the frightened sobbing of women, the strong curses of terrified men, the wailing of little children, blending with the hurried trampling of innumerable feet. Suddenly across the darkness flamed a blood-red, silent flash illumining the heavens from east to west. Against this lurid background loomed three crosses, stark and black. And now across the gloomy valleys sounded the sullen crash of rocks, the fall of giant trees, while the sick earth groaned aloud and trembled beneath its terrible burden.

Tor stood stock-still in the midst of the road. In that instant of frozen horror he comprehended what had happened. "Oh, my Father," he groaned, the foundations of his childish faith reeling with the reeling earth.

And the Omnipotent Love answered this feeble cry of the least of his children, even as it answered that far-reaching, agonized appeal which was sounding forth from Calvary. And so in a moment—or an eternity—the heavens cleared and the April sun shone brightly upon the crosses with their piteous burdens, upon the terror-stricken multitudes returning to doomed Jerusalem, upon riven tombs and shattered mountains, upon a little child, comforted of his Father, gazing with Christ-touched eyes upon the cross of his King.

They took away the body of Jesus before sunset, wrapping it in fine white linen and odorous spices, and laying it to rest in a garden hard by. Tor watched all, understanding little of the significance of the rock-hewn tomb, of the great stone before its door, of the Roman guard which was shortly stationed before the sealed sepulcher.

When all was finished the child returned to the city, sustained by some strange expectation which he could have explained to no one. As he would have entered the gate he came upon a woeful figure standing without and beating upon its breast. It was Chelluh, his wicked face disfigured with rage and pain. "My eyes," he groaned. "The sight of that accursed cross burnt them like a devouring flame." And so it was. And so will it ever be. He who can look upon that cross of agony without tears of love and pity, henceforth sees only the blackness of darkness. The eyes of his soul are withered.

Tor led the blind man to his old place by the gate, and fetched him his cup, his staff, and his water-gourd.

"Now go, little dog, buy me oil and wine," cried the beggar, with one of his frightful maledictions, "and return to me quickly, for I am devoured with this flame."

But Tor, looking upon him sorrowfully, knew that he could no more serve this evil master as in the old days. "I have done thus far for thee," he said in his clear childish voice, "because of the

King, my Master, and because of my Father in heaven. But I can no longer abide in thy presence. Farewell!" And with this he was gone, his naked feet making no sound upon the stones of the street.

Many days thereafter did Chelluh send forth his dolorous cry for alms in the doomed city of Jerusalem, for he lived until the terrible days of the Roman siege, perishing at last of hunger in his chosen place by the Damascus gate.

In the green garden-close, hard by Calvary, where the Roman guard paced ceaselessly back and forth before that silent tomb, Tor lingered, unnoticed and unafraid as the birds that flitted among the branches of the blossoming trees. It comforted him to be near the resting-place of his Master; and the lusty life of the young summer sent vague thrills of expectancy through his brown limbs, as he lay upon the warm earth watching the shifting leaf-shadows playing upon the sealed door of the sepulcher, and the slow-moving figures of the guard clad in the scarlet and gold of imperial Rome.

Toward midnight of the second night, when the great Passover moon rode high in the heavens and the garden slept in its silver light like the garden of a dream, the child slept, too, held in the soft clasp of a vision which laid cool fingers of delight on his drowsy lids. When he awoke he lay for a full minute staring into the branches of the olive tree above his head. The gray-green leaves were all alive with a tremulous motion in the fresh morning breeze; a newly-awakened bird trilled softly somewhere in the depths of the garden; the aromatic breath of serried lilies swept his cheek like a caress. It was happiness to have slept—to be once more awake. Then he remembered.

The Roman guard had disappeared; this much Tor perceived at a single glance. A second searching stare told him much more: the door of the tomb gaped wide, beside it stood a young man clad in white garments.

Tor approached this radiant figure unafraid. "Where is the man who opens eyes?" he asked quite simply, for the empty tomb appeared nothing strange to the child newly emerged from his healing dreams.

"He is not here," the young man made answer, with grave sweetness. "He is risen, as he said. Behold he goeth before you into Galilee; there shalt thou see him."

Tor opened wide eyes of rapture upon the angel. "My Master is alive!" he whispered to himself. "I shall see him."

He turned as if in a dream, his naked feet making no sound as he brushed, light as the dawn, past the ranks of lilies. There was a woman yonder. She was weeping with a smothered sound of long-drawn sobs. Tor laughed softly in his joy. "He is alive!" he repeated under his breath.

Then he saw with wonder that the woman was no longer alone. She was speaking to the Risen One, her voice wrenched with sobbing: "Sir, if thou hast borne him hence, tell me where thou hast laid him, and I will take him away."

The child's Christ-touched eyes knew him though the woman did not. He sank to his knees, his face shining with the dazzling light of the new day.

The Shadow of the Cross By Horatius Bonar

Oppress'd with noon-day's scorching heat,
To yonder cross I flee;
Beneath its shelter take my seat;
No shade like this for me!

Beneath that cross clear waters burst,
A fountain sparkling free;
And there I quench my desert thirst,
No spring like this for me!

A stranger here, I pitch my tent
Beneath this spreading tree;
Here shall my pilgrim life be spent;
No home like this for me!

For burdened ones a resting-place,
Beside that cross I see;
Here I cast off my weariness;
No rest like this for me!

Easter Songs

Sing the two songs together as a family. Discuss what the songs mean. If you are not familiar with these songs, sing some Easter songs that you know (look in a hymnal for ideas).

Alas! And Did My Savior Bleed?

Isaac Watts — Hugh Wilson

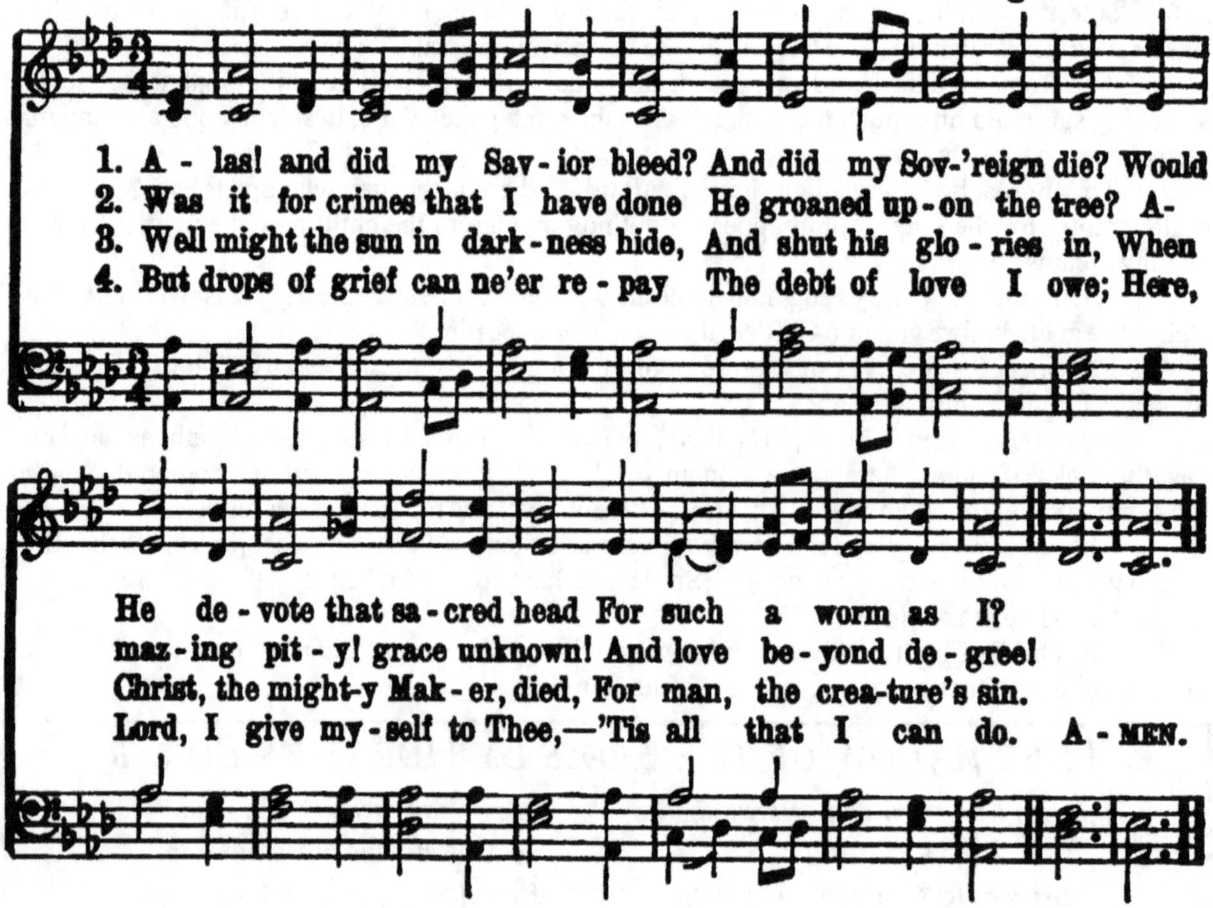

1. Alas! and did my Savior bleed? And did my Sov-'reign die? Would He devote that sacred head For such a worm as I?
2. Was it for crimes that I have done He groaned upon the tree? Amazing pity! grace unknown! And love beyond degree!
3. Well might the sun in darkness hide, And shut his glories in, When Christ, the mighty Maker, died, For man, the creature's sin.
4. But drops of grief can ne'er repay The debt of love I owe; Here, Lord, I give myself to Thee,—'Tis all that I can do. A-MEN.

Countdown to Easter — *Amy Puetz*

Palm Sunday

An Easter Snow Storm, Part 1
A Story of Russian Life, Founded on Fact
By P. Kitty Koudacheff

*I*t was a dull, lead-colored morning in March. The snow still covered the ground, and the small village of Viska lay cozily wrapped in its soft white covering, as if fast asleep.

Some croakers, casting dubious glances eastward up at the sky, and foretelling a heavy fall of snow, looked to their cattle, brought in more fuel, piled up the fire, and grumbled at what they called a "White Easter." It was the end of Holy Week, and most Russian housewives were busily employed baking, roasting, dyeing eggs, and generally preparing for the great feast. For in Russia, during the seven weeks of Lent, a severe fasting is strictly observed—that is, an abstinence from all but fish and vegetable products, even butter being forbidden; and it is the custom to prepare a great treat wherewith to greet Easter, or the Great Day, as it is generally called in Southern or Small Russia.

There were busy hands in every house in Viska on that Friday morning in Lent; even the small children helped. What with running errands, washing the raisins, dyeing the eggs crimson, purple, and yellow—what with getting the dye all over their hands and faces, and then scrubbing each other clean again, there was a great deal of work to be got through, both for great and small. Widow Smirnoff alone seemed to be idle. Her cleanly swept hearth showed no sign of either baking or cooking, and she seemed making ready to go on some distant errand. Her sheepskin coat, tightly bound with a green sash around her waist, her thick felt top-boots on, she was just in the act of slinging a large bundle over her arm, when Maxim, her rosy-cheeked, five-year-old boy, ventured one last appeal that he might accompany her.

"Oh, Mother, do take me with you! I can walk ten *versts* [a versts is nearly two thirds of a mile] quite easily in my little felt boots. I promise not to get tired, and I'd feel so lonely all by myself without you."

"But, *goloubtchick* [little dove], you will not be alone. You will spend the day at neighbor Petroff's. You will help them with the eggs, and I'll be back by night."

"No, no, Mother; I cannot stay. They all tease me, and ask why I do not color my own eggs, and why we are so poor. And they want to know what you have baked and prepared for the Great Day; and—and—" tears were glistening in the big brown eyes, and the poor mother felt very sorry for his childish trouble—"and you know, Mamma, if I go with you, we can pass the night at good old Trina's, and start early tomorrow for home, and be here in time to get all the good things ready; and I should be so happy—so happy!"

The pleading eyes were looking up into hers, and the mother's heart was melted.

"Well, then, by spending the night at Trina's I suppose you could manage the ten versts, little boy. So get on your things, and we'll start at once."

A quarter of an hour later, mother and son were trudging bravely through the snow, and out of the village, along the straight white road, edged here and there by deep ditches. They just stopped a moment on their way out to say a few words to old Stepan.

"Oh, ho! So the youngster goes with you today, neighbor?" said he. "Won't it be too much for his short legs?"

"We'll stay at Mirgorod over night, Stepan, and be back by tomorrow noon. Be sure you have those eggs and things ready against the time we pass."

"All right, Dame. By the by, I shall possibly be going to Mirgorod myself tomorrow morning, so I can give you a lift home in my sleigh. Good-day to you, and good luck selling your boublicks!"

Now, the contents of the bundle carried by Widow Smirnoff would have surprised young Americans if they had seen it. It was a quantity of hard-baked biscuits, or rather bread, shaped like rings about the size of large bracelets, and strung, some ten or twelve together, on bits of yarn. Of these giant necklaces she carried some two or three dozen, carefully wrapped up in a clean white cloth. These boublicks are a very popular accompaniment to tea; and though they are far and widely known, it is not every one who can make them the right way.

I have but a vague idea concerning their manufacture, and all I know is that they are made without any leaven, and first boiled in water and then baked, which gives them a crisp exterior, and insures their remaining fresh and good to eat for a whole fortnight.

It is quite a specialty, knowing how to make them; and Widow Smirnoff possessed this knowledge to a high degree. Her boublicks were renowned far and near; and since her husband's death she had baked and sold them, and with an odd job now and then, she was living and bringing up her little boy on the earnings of this industry. For she was very poor. She was not of the village where they lived, but had settled there with her husband when Maxim was but a baby—the husband working as farm laborer. When he died she had stayed on, renting a small cottage, selling her boublicks, and trying hard to earn enough money to take her and her child back to her own distant home on the Volga.

That is why there was no baking nor cooking going on at their home, and why she was trudging toward Mirgorod, a small garrison-town— rather village than town— with her bundle over her arm. The officers and men were her chief customers; but the winter had been so severe this year that she had not been able to walk over very often: so her purse was empty, and unless this time she sold her whole stock, little Maxim would have to do without his Easter treat.

On and on they walked, the boy insisting on helping his mother, and carrying a string or two of boublicks slung over his shoulder. Sometimes he would beg her to hold them a minute, while he slapped his hands together till he made the fingers tingle; and then, bravely taking his load up again, and holding on to his mother's sheepskin, he would babble away, in his cheerful, childish fashion, of all he would be and do when he grew up to be a man.

They had been walking for a long time, it seemed to Maxim, but he was not tired—not he! He only wondered why his mother had suddenly become silent; why she was forever looking up to the sky, with an anxious expression on her face; and why she took hold of his hand and held it so tight. Then it began to snow; and it snowed in such a funny, crazy sort of way, Maxim thought. It first blew into his face; then from behind; then again it seemed snowing from down below, the flakes flying up his nose and making him sneeze—and all the while his mother's hand closed tighter and tighter over his small fingers.

"I can't see my way, mother," said he, at last. "The snow is coming from all sides at once; and you know, dear, I am not really tired a bit, but I should so like to take just a wee bit of rest. I think I should walk quicker after, if I did."

The widow did not answer, but, stooping down, she took her boy in her arms, and silently plodded on through the ever-thickening snowstorm. She did not seem to mind the added weight, but hurried on. Little Maxim's head gradually bent lower and lower, till it lay at last on her shoulder.

"Thank you, mother; this is good. I shall be all right in a minute, for I am not really tired, only just a little bit sleepy," he said.

And still she hurried on. She must be near her journey's end, surely! They had been walking three hours at least, and the steeple of Mirgorod would probably have been in view were it not for the storm. She could not have missed her way; she knew it so well, and besides, were there not ditches nearly all along the road? True, the snow was blowing furiously into her face, but still she could not have passed over the ditch without falling in.

On and on she plodded. The wind grew ever fiercer; the snow was whirling and drifting, then flying high up from the ground again in a kind of twirling, revolving column; then suddenly careering along the white surface, to be finally merged into another snow-laden gust, and piled up high against any obstruction it might chance to meet in its wild race. The poor mother struggled through the blinding snow, little Maxim fast asleep on her shoulder. What with the weight in her arms, the howling of the wind, and the furiously raging storm around her, and the faintness and dizziness she had been trying to conquer, the widow was beginning to lose heart, when suddenly her foot slipped, and she felt herself sliding down a soft, sloping surface.

"Strange!" she muttered; "there ought not to be any ditch on this side of the road. I must have mistaken my way, after all, but, anyhow, we'll be more sheltered down here, and in an hour or so the storm is sure to calm down. I may as well rest a bit."

So she carefully put down her bundle of boublicks, hollowed out a kind of niche, something like an arm-chair, in the snow, and she dropped down into this seat, and fell to thinking of when she should get to Mirgorod; and how little Maxim would manage the rest of the way; and whether neighbor Stepan would have the things in readiness for her next morning; and how strange that such a storm should have come on in March; and how foolish of her to have taken Maxim; and then—and then—

To be continued!

The Splendor of the Lilies
By Margaret Elizabeth Munson Sangster

Oh, rare as the splendor of lilies,
And sweet as the violet's breath,
Comes the jubilant morning of Easter,
The triumph of life over death;
And fresh from the earth's quickened bosom
Full baskets of flowers we bring,
And scatter their satin soft petals
To carpet a path for our King.

In the countless green blades of the meadow,
The sheen of the daffodil's gold,
In the tremulous blue on the mountains,
The opaline mist on the wold,
In the tinkle of brooks through the pasture,
The river's strong sweep to the sea,
Are signs of the day that is hasting
In gladness to you and to me.

Oh, dawn in thy splendor of lilies,
Thy fluttering violet breath,
Oh, jubilant morning of Easter,
Thou triumph of life over death!
Then fresh from the earth's quickened bosom
Full baskets of flowers we bring,
And scatter their satin soft petals
To carpet a path for our King.

Easter Riddles

How Many Eggs?
By Melville De Lancey Landon and Mark Twain

A country woman carrying eggs to a garrison had three guards to pass, she sold at the first, half the number she had, and half an egg more; at the second, half of what remained and half an egg more; at the third half of the remainder and half an egg more. When she arrived at the market place she had thirty-six eggs; how many had she at first?

Solution. By taking the greater part of an odd number we take the exact ½ an egg more, therefore the woman had, before she passed the last guard, seventy-three eggs; in like manner before she passed the second guard she had 147; and before she came to the first guard she had 295 eggs.

Jokes and Riddles
By Melville De Lancey Landon and Mark Twain

When is a baker like a beggar?
When he kneads bread.

When is dough like the sun?
When it rises it is light.

When is a chimney like a chicken?
When it is a little foul (fowl).

No doors there are in this strong hold
Yet thieves break in and steal the gold.
(An Egg)

Easter Craft

Easter Bookmarks By Amy Puetz

You will need:
Colored cardstock or paper   Scissors

1. Copy the bookmarks on the next page onto colored cardstock or paper.

2. Cut them out. They may be laminated with contact paper if desired.

Countdown to Easter   Amy Puetz

Watch and pray, that ye enter not into temptation: the spirit indeed is willing, but the flesh is weak.
Matthew 26:41

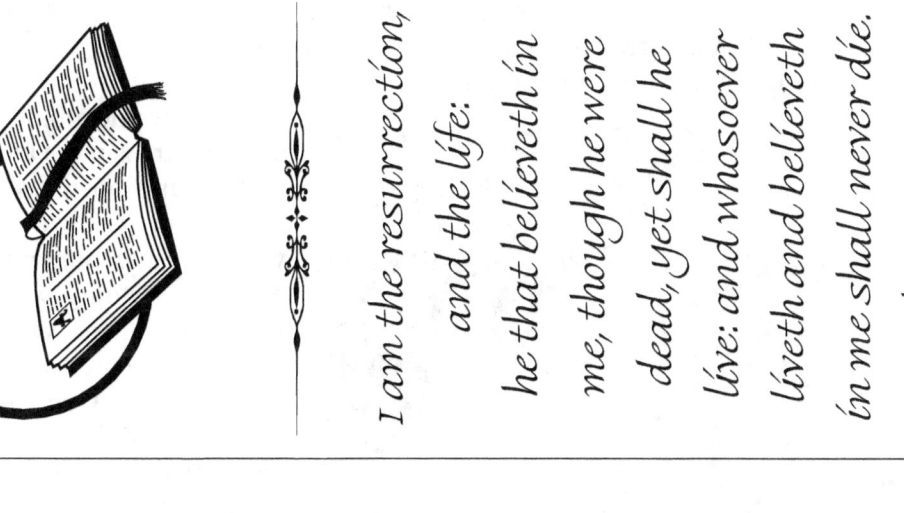

I am the resurrection, and the life: he that believeth in me, though he were dead, yet shall he live: and whosoever liveth and believeth in me shall never die.
John 11:25-26

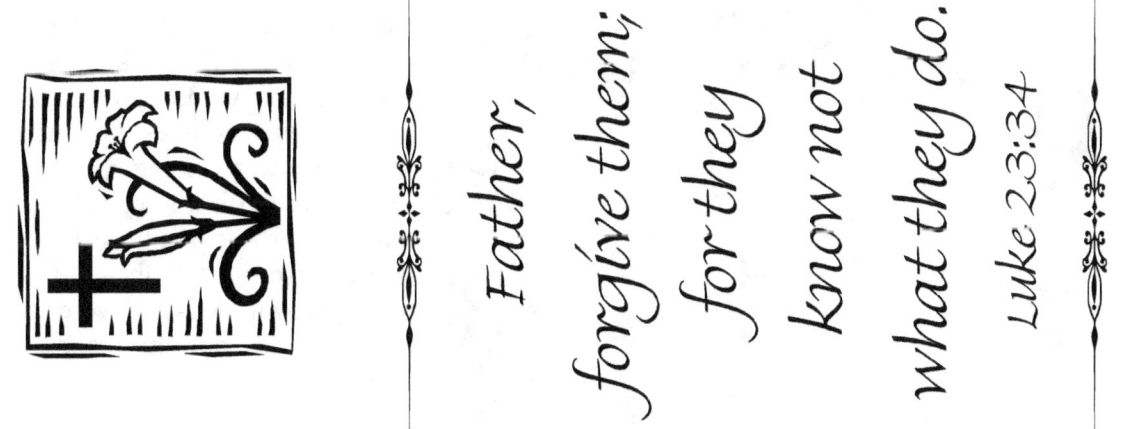

Father, forgive them; for they know not what they do.
Luke 23:34

How a Little Brown Bulb Became an Easter Lily
By Florence Ursula Palmer

Many weeks ago a little brown house like this seed was put into a large crock of earth, and the crock set in a sunny corner of a big greenhouse. The sunshine came through the glass roof, the house was kept warm, and every day the secret in the brown house could hear the trickling of water, and feel something coming down through the dirt.

Days came and went, wintry days, and then warm days. The sunbeams that fell on the greenhouse roof, and down on the dirt in the crock, never dreamed of the secret that was working so hard to free itself, to get out of the brown house, and up into the light. The days grew longer, and at last the brown house could hold it no longer. It burst the walls.

Slowly it rose, inch by inch it came up through the dirt to the light, where the blossoms of the plants in the greenhouse were watching to see it. Its roots had spread out in the dirt, and its straight stalk was growing up, up. Leaves were growing around it.

Now the robins were coming back, the trees were unfolding their leaflets, and on the stem that had come from the brown house, and was standing among the green leaves, something was opening. It was white. There were six leaflets, and in the center stems powdered with yellow. One by one they unfolded, and then a strange, sweet odor filled the air. It was Easter morning. Out of the brown house had risen a lily, pure white—a lily to add its joy to that glad Easter morn.

The lily looked around. Through the window it could see the green grass, the trees, the birds. All the world was waking up. The early blossoms, daffodils and violets were out. They had come from seeds—as the lily from the bulb—had grown out of brown seeds and were now up in the light, out in this big new world.

Monday of Passion Week

An Easter Snow Storm, Part 2
A Story of Russian Life, Founded on Fact
By P. Kitty Koudacheff

"Mother, wake up! Mother, I am afraid! Where are we?" And the little boy wriggled in her arms. "Are we at Mirgorod, Mother,—and how did we get here?"

With a start, the widow Smirnoff opened her eyes, but all around was dark.

"I must have fallen asleep, *douchka* [little soul]," she answered; "But how could I have slept so long? The storm is over, however; I do not hear it roar, and the air seems quite warm."

She tried to get up, but knocked her head against something. Trying to move her arms, she encountered the same soft barrier all around her. On every side, and above her head, her hands touched the cool snowy walls. She shuddered as the thought flashed through her head that they were buried alive! With a beating heart the widow again and again moved her hands carefully in all directions, meeting ever the same cool surface, till, sick at heart, she had to own the terrible truth—"Snowed in!"

When she had fallen asleep it had kept on snowing, now gently sweeping over them, now drifting with a gust of wind; and so regularly had the snow been swept into the ditch and against its sides, that it ended by filling the ditch, and covering them entirely. The warmth of their breath and bodies had thawed the snow about their heads; but the white walls, rising gradually higher and higher, had met at last overhead, roofing them in, so to say, as the storm raged on.

Imagine the mother's despair! She tried to stand up, but the weight of the snow was too great. The cramped position she was in was hard to endure; but, happily, neither she nor little Maxim was cold. It is always quite warm under a thick coating of snow, and, refreshed by his sleep, the little fellow was feeling quite cheerful. When the widow explained where and how they were situated, and that they should probably have to remain snowed up for some hours, he greatly relieved her anxieties by proving himself to be a true "son of the steppes," hardy and brave under difficulties.

He was in a curious position and experiencing something quite new; but then, was not his mother with him, and had not she always proved able to help him through all his difficulties and struggles in life? He was very hungry, though, and gladly set to nibbling at a boublick, while his mother began working for their release. Roadside ditches in Russia are generally very deep, for most of the roads being unpaved; the ditches must hold great quantities of water produced by autumn rains and the thawing of the snow in spring. These ditches, therefore, sometimes reach five or six feet in depth, and are about four feet wide at the top, growing narrower toward the bottom. They are bordered sometimes by a hedge of thistles or other wild, brushy growth, which helps to arrest the snow, and after a storm they usually look like long, white walls.

The only way to get out was to burrow out, and this the widow set to work to do, scooping the snow with her hands. This proved slow work at best, as she had to rest often; and after a time she again took little Maxim in her arms, and told him he was a brave boy, and must now try and take some rest. She knew there could be no danger of a chill for the child sleeping under the snow. It was quite warm, and she hoped that a few hours' more work, when perfectly rested, would bring them to the surface again.

"Mother, I wonder is it tomorrow yet?" asked Maxim, with a puzzled intonation in his voice; "We have been down here so long, and we have slept and worked a good deal, and I feel quite mixed in my head. Oh, I only hope it is not Easter yet! Fancy how sad it would be, spending it here, in this old ditch, and missing the night service at church, and the singing, and the game of eggs, and all the glorious pleasures of the Great Day! I do not mind staying here with you, Mother, but wouldn't it be dreadful to miss it all!"

"Come, goloubtchick, do not grieve! I am sure we shall soon be free; and if we work hard, who knows but we may still sell our boublicks in Mirgorod, and be at home again in time for Easter?" So they said their prayers together, as they had done every night ever since Maxim first learned to speak, and the little boy was soon sleeping peacefully in his mother's arms. But it was long before the widow, though spent with her late exertions and the anxiety she had hidden from her boy, could follow his example. What if more snow fell, followed by a severe frost, as sometimes will happen in March, just before the real thawing sets in? They had boublicks enough to last them many days, but would her strength hold out? And if she gave way, what would become of Maxim? So she thought and thought, until at last her weary eyelids closed, and she, too, was safe in the Land of Nod.

She was roused from her sleep by a regular thump, thump, thump, as of a shovel at work overhead. She knew, then, that rescue was at hand, and seizing Maxim, who had also been awakened, in her arms, she lifted him on to her shoulder, bidding him ply his hands sturdily at the roof of their prison. Great was the boy's impatience to be free, and scarcely did he feel himself lifted up, than he began banging his head against the snow, and exclaiming: "Come down, old wretch! You've had us locked up long enough! Take that, and that!" A white avalanche suddenly rushed down, nearly knocking Maxim off his perch, going down his throat, and into his eyes, and nearly choking him; and with it—oh, welcome sight! A stream of sunshine!

Widow Smirnoff had to shut her eyes a moment to avoid the welcome glare, but Maxim's shrill "Hurrah!" made her look up next moment, to see him bodily snatched out of her arms, and safely deposited on the road beyond; then all was dark again. When she recovered from her swoon, it was to find herself lying on the road, just by the side of the ditch, with old Stepan's friendly face beaming over her, while Maxim was capering wildly around.

"So, neighbor, is that the way you manage your affairs?" he asked, when she was quite herself again. "Well, well, everyone to his taste, but I should have preferred spending the night at old Trina's, had I been you! And you have not sold a single boublick, I declare!" as he caught sight of the bundle, half buried in snow at the bottom of the ditch. Thereupon he scrambled down, and brought it up, still grumbling as he gave it a shake or two. But he was very kind, with all that, and helped the widow and Maxim into his sleigh.

"Of all places to be snowed up in, I should just like to know why you chose this, almost in the streets of Mirgorod!" he continued; and, sure enough, the first houses of the small town were only about a stone's throw from their white prison.

"Now, I suppose I shall have to turn back into town again, so as to let you dispose of your goods! Always the same, you women-folk! You'll be getting snowed up in your own yard next time, I warrant!"

With these words, he turned his horse's head toward the officers' quarters; but before they entered the principal street they were met by a whole party of men with shovels and spades coming toward them.

"All right!" shouted Stepan, triumphantly waving his whip, as he caught sight of them. "I've got them safe! They're both all right!"

The men gave a cheer, and then came a whole string of questions and answers, all jumbled together, and hard to make head or tail of in the general din. When the widow's story was told, she heard how old Stepan had stopped for her that morning at Trina's, and, on being told that she had not been there, had hastened over to the barracks. She had neither been seen nor heard of there, whereupon, madly rushing to those of the inhabitants he knew, and summoning them all to lend a hand in the search, he had set off in advance with his sleigh and a shovel. Attracted by some inequalities on the surface of the snow beside the ditch, he had begun shoveling away, and with what happy result has been seen.

All Mirgorod was on foot to welcome the rescued pair, and though the boublicks were not very good, after twenty-four hours spent in the snow, every one of them was bought, and late in the afternoon Maxim and his mother were being driven swiftly over the same road they had plodded along with such difficulty the day before.

On reaching home, they found that neighbor Stepan had been, before them; on the table, all in a row, stood, first, a high, tower-shaped cake with a sugar coating, and a big paper flower stuck on the top. Beside it was the pascha, or Easter cheese, with fat raisins to be seen sticking out here and there; there was also a large piece of bacon, and last, but not least, a plateful of bright red and yellow hard-boiled eggs!

How Maxim clapped his little hands for joy, and how he danced round and round the table in an ecstasy of delight, until he fell asleep on the wooden settee, holding an egg in each hand, his glossy curls resting on his arms!

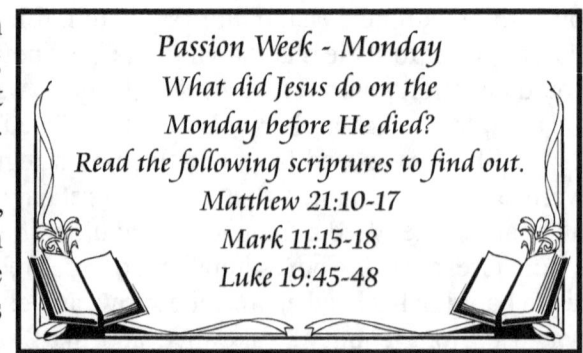

Passion Week - Monday
What did Jesus do on the Monday before He died?
Read the following scriptures to find out.
Matthew 21:10-17
Mark 11:15-18
Luke 19:45-48

His mother put him to bed without waking him, and he slept right through the night and late into Easter morning, while his mother gave thanks with a heart overflowing with a great love and gratitude for their preservation.

THE TWO THIEVES BY MRS. JAMESON

We know from Josephus the historian, that about this time Palestine was infested by bands of robbers. There is an ancient tradition, that when the Holy Family, travelling through hidden paths and solitary defiles, had passed Jerusalem, and were descending into the plains of Syria, they encountered certain thieves who fell upon them; and one of them would have maltreated and plundered them; but his comrade interfered, and said, 'Suffer them, I beseech thee, to go in peace, and I will give thee forty groats, and likewise my girdle;' which offer being accepted, the merciful robber led the Holy Travelers to his stronghold on the rock, and gave them lodging for the night. And Mary said to him, 'The Lord God will receive thee to his right hand, and grant the pardon of thy sins!' And it was so: for in after times these two thieves were crucified with Christ, one on the right hand, and one on the left; and the merciful thief went with the Savior into Paradise.

Easter Eggs

Decorate Easter Eggs By Amy Puetz

Hard boil the eggs first. To do this place eggs in a pan and cover with cold water. On high, bring water to the boiling point and reduce the heat to low. Cover and cook eggs for 20 minutes. Place in cold water to cool.

After the eggs are cool the fun begins! There are kits that can be purchased at the grocery store, or you can make your own dyes.

To make your own dye put water, white vinegar, and food coloring in a bowl or cup that is large enough to hold an egg. Have one bowl for each color. To dye an egg, put it in a bowl and let it set until it has reached the desired color. Don't leave it in too long, though, or the vinegar will eat through the egg shell. Let the dye dry before putting the egg in another color.

Color the eggs with crayons. This may be done before the egg is put in the dye since the dye will not penetrate through the crayon. You may also draw on the egg after it has been dyed. To paint on the eggs use diluted food coloring and a new paint brush or cotton swab.

Glue buttons, sequins or other decorations on the eggs. Pretty stickers also look nice. The ideas are limitless. Have fun!

Tuesday of Passion Week

A Lesson of Faith
By Mrs. Julia Cowles

A mild, green caterpillar was one day strolling about on a cabbage leaf, when there settled beside her a beautiful Butterfly.

The Butterfly fluttered her wings feebly, and seemed very ill.

"I feel very strange and dizzy," said the Butterfly, addressing the Caterpillar, "and I am sure that I have but a little while to live. But I have just laid some butterfly eggs on this cabbage leaf, and if I die there will be no one to care for my baby butterflies. I must hire a nurse for them at once, but I cannot go far to seek one. May I hire you as nurse, kind Caterpillar? I will pay you with gold dust from my wings."

Then, before the surprised Caterpillar could reply, the Butterfly went on, "Of course you must not feed them on the coarse cabbage leaves which are your food. Young butterflies must be fed upon early dew and the honey of flowers. And at first, oh, good Caterpillar, they must not be allowed to fly far, for their wings will not be strong. It is sad that you cannot fly yourself. But I am sure you will be kind, and will do the best you can."

With that the poor Butterfly drooped her wings and died, and the Caterpillar had no chance to so much as say "Yes," or "No."

"Dear me!" she exclaimed, as she looked at the butterfly eggs beside her, "what sort of a nurse will I make for a group of happy young butterflies? Much attention they will pay to the advice of a plain caterpillar like me. But I shall have to do the best that I can," she added. And all that night she walked around and around the butterfly eggs to see that no harm came to them.

"I wish that I had someone wiser than myself to consult with," she said to herself next morning. "I might talk it over with the house dog. But, no," she added hastily, "he is kind, but big and rough, and one brush of his tail would whisk all the eggs off the cabbage leaf.

"There is Tom Cat," she went on, after thinking a few moments, "but he is lazy and selfish, and he would not give himself the trouble to think about butterfly eggs.

"Ah, but there's the Lark!" she exclaimed at length. "He flies far up into the heavens and perhaps he knows more than we creatures that live upon the earth. I'll ask him." So the Caterpillar sent a message to the Lark, who lived in a neighboring cornfield, and she told him all her troubles.

"And I want to know how I, a poor crawling Caterpillar, am to feed and care for a family of beautiful young butterflies. Could you find out for me the next time you fly away up into the blue heavens?"

"Perhaps I can," said the Lark, and off he flew. Higher and higher he winged his way until the poor, crawling Caterpillar could not even hear his song, to say nothing of seeing him. After a very long time—at least it seemed so to the Caterpillar, who, in her odd, lumbering way, kept walking around and around the butterfly eggs—the Lark came back.

First, she could hear his song away up in the heavens. Then it sounded nearer and nearer, till he alighted close beside her and began to speak.

"I found out many wonderful things," he said. "But if I tell them to you, you will not believe me."

"Oh, yes I will," answered the Caterpillar hastily, "I believe everything I am told."

"Well, then," said the Lark, "the first thing I found out was that the butterfly eggs will turn into little green caterpillars, just like yourself, and that they will eat cabbage leaves just as you do."

"Wretch!" exclaimed the Caterpillar, bristling with indignation. "Why do you come and mock me with such a story as that? I thought you would be kind, and would try to help me."

"So I would," answered the Lark, "but I told you, you would not believe me," and with that he flew away to the cornfield.

"Dear me," said the Caterpillar, sorrowfully. "When the Lark flies so far up into the heavens I should not think he would come back to us poor creatures with such a silly tale. And I needed help so badly."

"I would help you if you would only believe me," said the Lark, flying down to the cabbage patch once more. "I have wonderful things to tell you, if you would only have faith in me and trust in what I say."

"And you are not making fun of me?" asked the Caterpillar.

"Of course not," answered the Lark.

"But you tell me such impossible things!"

"If you could fly with me and see the wonders that I see, here on earth, and away up in the blue sky, you would not say that anything was impossible," replied the Lark.

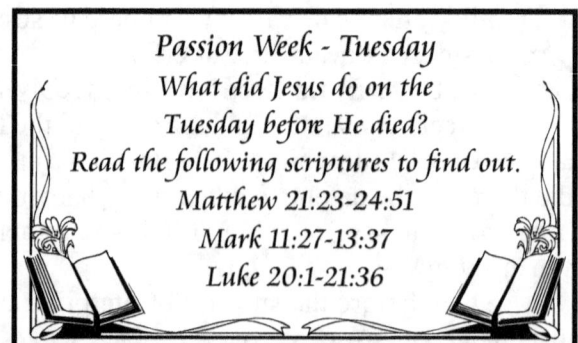

Passion Week - Tuesday
What did Jesus do on the Tuesday before He died?
Read the following scriptures to find out.
Matthew 21:23-24:51
Mark 11:27-13:37
Luke 20:1-21:36

"But," said the Caterpillar, "you tell me that these eggs will hatch out into caterpillars, and I know that their mother was a butterfly, for I saw her with my own eyes; and so of course they will be butterflies. How could they be anything else? I am sure I can reason that far, if I cannot fly."

"Very well," answered the Lark, "then I must leave you, though I have even more wonderful things that I could tell. But what comes to you from the heavens, you can only receive by faith, as I do. You cannot crawl around on your cabbage leaf and reason these things out."

"Oh, I do believe what I am told," repeated the Caterpillar—although she had just proved that it was not true—"at least," she added, "everything that is reasonable to believe. Pray tell me what else you learned."

"I learned," said the Lark, impressively, "that you will be a butterfly, yourself, someday."

"Now, indeed, you are making fun of me," exclaimed the Caterpillar, ready to cry with vexation and disappointment. But just at that moment she felt something brush against her side, and, turning her head, she looked in amazement at the cabbage leaf, for there, just coming out of the butterfly eggs, were eight or ten little green caterpillars—and they were no more than out of the eggs before they began eating the juicy leaf. Oh, how astonished and how ashamed the Caterpillar felt. What the Lark had said was true!

And then a very wonderful thought came to the poor, green Caterpillar. "If this part is true, it must all be true, and some day I shall be a butterfly."

She was so delighted that she began telling all her caterpillar friends about it—but they did not believe her any more than she had believed the Lark.

"But I know, I know," she kept saying to herself. And she never tired of hearing the Lark sing of the wonders of the earth below, and of the heavens above. All the time, the little green caterpillars on the leaf grew and thrived wonderfully, and the big green Caterpillar watched them and cared for them carefully every hour. One day the Caterpillar's friends gathered around her and said, very sorrowfully, "It is time for you to spin your chrysalis and die."

But the Caterpillar replied, "You mean that I shall soon be changed into a beautiful butterfly. How wonderful it will be."

And her friends looked at one another sadly and said, "She is quite out of her mind."

Then the Caterpillar spun her chrysalis and went to sleep. And by and by, when she awoke, oh, then she knew that what the Lark had learned in the heavens was true—for she was a beautiful butterfly, with gold dust on her wings.

Easter Egg Activities

Easter Egg Hunt By Ellye Howell Glover

No Easter-tide is complete for the children without an egg hunt. If the weather permits this should be out of doors. Hide eggs of all sizes and colors, hard-boiled, and candy ones, in every conceivable place. If the party is a large one there should be four prizes, one to the child getting the golden egg (gilded), one for finding the silver egg, one for finding the most and one for the child who finds the egg marked "third prize." The prizes should be some of the many Easter novelties, or candy boxes filled with candy eggs. A pot of jonquils or hyacinths is a suitable prize if the winner is about eight or ten years old. Serve ice cream, rabbit shaped cookies and bonbons. There is a very old game called "egg pick" that the children should play after the hunt. Use only hard-boiled eggs. A child who strikes out with his egg at one held by another child and whose egg breaks or cracks first wins the other egg. If there is a hill conveniently placed, or even a slight slant to the ground, there may be an egg-rolling on a small scale such as the children had in Washington at the White House for many years.

The Celebration of Easter By Ellye Howell Glover

The celebration of Easter is almost as universal as Christmas, and how children love it! All the symbols are so beautiful; and even the smallest child may be taught the wonderful significance of the resurrection as it comes to us with every return of spring.

There are many charming devices for entertainment to be given during Easter week, but the time-honored egg hunt is best loved by boys and girls. Let me tell of this original way of varying the hunt: Have all kinds of eggs, of candy, china, favor eggs, and the real fruit of the hen, gilded, silvered and colored. Then make a big score card and put up where it may easily be consulted. Place a value on the different eggs, a gold one to count twenty; silver, ten; blue ones, five; candy ones, four; the very smallest, one, etc. Then for very special prize favor eggs fifty will be the score. Give the guests baskets or silk bags for the spoils and have plenty of assistants to help the children add up their eggs correctly, each one to keep what he or she finds; and, besides, have rewards for the best scores. This will add zest to the hunt and take fully an hour. If the weather is fine some of the eggs might be hidden outdoors. The centerpiece for this party may be a huge egg in a nest of tinsel and imitation grass; on cracking the egg it will be found to contain an egg or Easter favor for each guest.

Easter Egg Games
By Lina Beard & Adelia Belle Beard

Press Release from 1897
THE EASTER EGG-ROLLING
CHILDREN SHAKE HANDS
WITH THE PRESIDENT

"The crowd in the White House grounds greatly increased yesterday afternoon, so that the grounds were literally packed with children. The crowd was the largest and best appearing that has collected there in many years. The President and Colonel Lamont watched the children for some time from the library window. At the President's reception at half-past one o'clock hundreds of children gave up their sport temporarily and thronged the East Room to shake hands with the President."

In the game they play at Washington, on the hills sloping from the White House, the child whose egg reaches the foot of the hill in an unbroken condition takes the one worsted in the journey down. Another game for two is played by knocking the eggs together; each child holds an egg firmly in his hand so that only the small end is visible, and then the two eggs are struck against each other until one is cracked, when the victorious player adds it to his stock.

Sometimes the egg which breaks another is called "the cock of one," and when it has broken two it is "cock of two," and so on. When an egg which is cock of one or more is broken, the number of trophies won by the victim is added to the score of the conquering egg and it becomes "cock of three" or more.

Here is a game which comes from Germany, and although in that country it is played exclusively by boys, there is no reason why the girls should not participate in it as well. Two baskets are necessary for this game, one large and shallow filled with soft shavings, the other shallow also, but smaller, and filled with eggs. The plan of the game is that one player is to run a given distance, while another safely throws the eggs from one basket to the other, she who completes her task first being the winner. When the baskets are prepared, and the distance the eggs are to be thrown decided upon, the two contestants draw lots to determine who shall run and who shall throw. This settled, the player who throws takes the basket of eggs, and one after another quickly tosses them the length of the course and into the basket of shavings, which is placed on the ground at the end of the course opposite the thrower. In Germany this basket is held by an assistant, but anyone occupying that position might receive some severe blows from the hard eggs thrown by unpracticed hands, and it answers the purpose just as well to place the basket on the ground. Meantime the other player runs the distance (decided beforehand) to an appointed goal, marks it as a proof of having touched it, and should she succeed in returning before all the eggs are thrown, the victory and prize are her reward; otherwise they belong to the thrower.

The game finished, a prize is presented to the successful contestant. Should any of the eggs pitched by the thrower fail to light in the basket, they must be gathered up and thrown again before the runner returns, as the eggs must all be in the basket before the thrower wins the game.

"Bunching eggs" comes from Ireland, and is played in very much the same manner as the game played with a slate and pencil, and known to all children as "tit, tat, toe, three in a row." A pan or large dish filled with sand or sawdust is set upon a table, around which the children stand, each supplied with eggs; the eggs of each player must be all of one color, and unlike those of any other player. The object of the game is for each player to so place her eggs, standing them upright in the sand, or sawdust, as to bring five in a row touching each other.

In turn each player puts down an egg, sometimes filling out a row for herself, at others cutting off the line of an opponent; and the one who first succeeds in obtaining the desired row sings out—

"The raven, chough, and crow,
Say five in a row."

Another pretty game from Ireland called "Touch" is played in the following manner:

Six eggs of the different colors—green, red, black, blue, white, and gold are placed in a row in the sand used for the other game. One of the players is blindfolded and given a light wand or stick, with which she must touch one of the eggs, while at the same time she recites these lines:

Peggy, Patrick, Mike, and Meg,
See me touch my Easter egg;
Green, and red, and black, and blue,
Count for six, five, four, and two.
If I touch an egg of white,
A forfeit then will be your right;
If I touch an egg of gold,
It is mine to have and hold.

As is told in the rhyme, the eggs each have a different value. Green counts six; red, five; black, four; and blue, two; and the gold egg is worth more than all put together, for when a player touches that, she wins the game and a forfeit of an egg from each of the other players. The white egg is worth less than nothing, since it not only has no value but whoever touches it with the wand must pay a forfeit.

Each player is in turn blindfolded and makes her trial, keeping account of the value of the eggs she has touched. When the sum of twenty has been reached by anyone the game is ended, without the aid of the gold egg. The position of the eggs are changed after each trial, that the person about to touch them may not know where it is best to place her wand.

Wednesday of Passion Week

The Nazarene
By Lew Wallace
From Ben-Hur, book eighth, chapter III

The first person to go out of the city upon the opening of the Sheep's Gate next morning was Amrah, basket on arm. No questions were asked her by the keepers, since the morning itself had not been more regular in coming than she; they knew her somebody's faithful servant, and that was enough for them.

Down the eastern valley she took her way. The side of Olivet, darkly green, was spotted with white tents recently put up by people attending the feasts; the hour, however, was too early for the strangers to be abroad; still, had it not been so, no one would have troubled her. Past Gethsemane; past the tombs at the meeting of the Bethany roads; past the sepulchral village of Siloam she went. Occasionally the decrepit little body staggered; once she sat down to get her breath; rising shortly, she struggled on with renewed haste. The great rocks on either hand, if they had had ears, might have heard her mutter to herself; could they have seen, it would have been to observe how frequently she looked up over the Mount, reproving the dawn for its promptness; if it had been possible for them to gossip, not improbably they would have said to each other, "Our friend is in a hurry this morning; the mouths she goes to feed must be very hungry."

When at last she reached the King's Garden she slackened her gait; for then the grim city of the lepers was in view, extending far round the pitted south hill of Hinnom.

As the reader must by this time have surmised, she was going to her mistress, whose tomb, it will be remembered, overlooked the well En-Rogel.

Early as it was, the unhappy woman was up and sitting outside, leaving Tirzah asleep within. The course of the malady had been terribly swift in the three years. Conscious of her appearance, with the refined instincts of her nature, she kept her whole person habitually covered. Seldom as possible she permitted even Tirzah to see her.

This morning she was taking the air with bared head, knowing there was no one to be shocked by the exposure. The light was not full, but enough to show the ravages to which she had been subject. Her hair was snow-white and unmanageably coarse, falling over her back and shoulders like so much silver wire. The eyelids, the lips, the nostrils, the flesh of the cheeks, were either gone or reduced to fetid rawness. The neck was a mass of ash-colored scales. One hand lay outside the folds of her habit rigid as that of a skeleton; the nails had been eaten away; the joints of the fingers, if not bare to the bone, were swollen knots crusted with red secretion. Head, face, neck, and hand indicated all too plainly the condition of the whole body. Seeing her thus, it was easy to understand how the once fair widow of the princely Hur had been able to maintain her incognito so well through such a period of years.

When the sun would gild the crest of Olivet and the Mount of Offence with light sharper and more brilliant in that old land than in the West, she knew Amrah would come, first to the well, then to a stone midway the well and the foot of the hill on which she had her abode, and that the good servant would there deposit the food she carried in the basket, and fill the water-jar afresh for the day. Of her former plentitude of happiness, that brief visit was all that remained to the unfortunate. She could then ask about her son, and be told of his welfare, with such bits of news concerning him as the messenger could glean. Usually the information was meagre enough, yet comforting; at times she heard he was at home; then she would issue from her dreary cell at break of day, and sit till noon, and from noon to set of sun, a motionless figure draped in white, looking, statue-like, invariably to one point—over the Temple to the spot under the rounded sky where the old house stood, dear in memory, and dearer because he was there. Nothing else was left her. Tirzah she counted of the dead; and as for herself, she simply waited the end, knowing every hour of life was an hour of dying—happily, of painless dying.

The things of nature about the hill to keep her sensitive to the world's attractions were wretchedly scant; beasts and birds avoided the place as if they knew its history and present use; every green thing perished in its first season; the winds warred upon the shrubs and venturous grasses, leaving to drought such as they could not uproot. Look where she would, the view was made depressingly suggestive by tombs—tombs above her, tombs below, tombs opposite her own tomb—all now freshly whitened in warning to visiting pilgrims. In the sky—clear, fair, inviting—one would think she might have found some relief to her ache of mind; but, alas! In making the beautiful elsewhere the sun served her never so unfriendly—it did but disclose her growing hideousness. But for the sun she would not have been the horror she was to herself, nor been waked so cruelly from dreams of Tirzah as she used to be. The gift of seeing can be sometimes a dreadful curse.

Does one ask why she did not make an end to her sufferings?

The Law forbade her!

A Gentile may smile at the answer; but so will not a son of Israel.

While she sat there peopling the dusky solitude with thoughts even more cheerless, suddenly a woman came up the hill staggering and spent with exertion.

The widow arose hastily, and covering her head, cried, in a voice unnaturally harsh, "Unclean, unclean!"

In a moment, heedless of the notice, Amrah was at her feet. All the long-pent love of the simple creature burst forth: with tears and passionate exclamations she kissed her mistress's garments, and for a while the latter strove to escape from her; then, seeing she could not, she waited till the violence of the paroxysm was over.

"What have you done, Amrah?" she said. "Is it by such disobedience you prove your love for us? Wicked woman! You are lost; and he—your master—you can never, never go back to him."

Amrah grovelled sobbing in the dust.

"The ban of the Law is upon you, too; you cannot return to Jerusalem. What will become of us? Who will bring us bread? O wicked, wicked Amrah! We are all, all undone alike!"

"Mercy, mercy!" Amrah answered from the ground.

"You should have been merciful to yourself, and by so doing been most merciful to us. Now where can we fly? There is no one to help us. O false servant! The wrath of the Lord was already too heavy upon us."

Here Tirzah, awakened by the noise, appeared at the door of the tomb. The pen shrinks from the picture she presented. In the half-clad apparition, patched with scales, lividly seamed, nearly blind, its limbs and extremities swollen to grotesque largeness, familiar eyes however sharpened by love could not have recognized the creature of childish grace and purity we first beheld her.

"Is it Amrah, mother?"

The servant tried to crawl to her also.

"Stay, Amrah!" the widow cried, imperiously. "I forbid you touching her. Rise, and get you gone before any at the well see you here. Nay, I forgot—it is too late! You must remain now and share our doom. Rise, I say!"

Amrah rose to her knees, and said, brokenly and with clasped hands, "O good mistress! I am not false—I am not wicked. I bring you good tidings."

"Of Judah?" and as she spoke, the widow half withdrew the cloth from her head.

"There is a wonderful man," Amrah continued, "who has power to cure you. He speaks a word, and the sick are made well, and even the dead come to life. I have come to take you to him."

"Poor Amrah!" said Tirzah, compassionately.

"No," cried Amrah, detecting the doubt underlying the expression—"no, as the Lord lives, even the Lord of Israel, my God as well as yours, I speak the truth. Go with me, I pray, and lose no time. This morning he will pass by on his way to the city. See! The day is at hand. Take the food here—eat, and let us go."

The mother listened eagerly. Not unlikely she had heard of the wonderful man, for by this time his fame had penetrated every nook in the land.

"Who is he?" she asked.

"A Nazarene."

"Who told you about him?"

"Judah."

"Judah told you? Is he at home?"

"He came last night."

The widow, trying to still the beating of her heart, was silent awhile.

"Did Judah send you to tell us this?" she next asked.

"No. He believes you dead."

"There was a prophet once who cured a leper," the mother said thoughtfully to Tirzah; "but he had his power from God." Then addressing Amrah, she asked, "How does my son know this man so possessed?"

"He was traveling with him, and heard the lepers call, and saw them go away well. First there was one man; then there were ten; and they were all made whole."

The elder listener was silent again. The skeleton hand shook. We may believe she was struggling to give the story the sanction of faith, which is always an absolutist in demand, and that it was with her as with the men of the day, eye-witnesses of what was done by the Christ, as well as the myriads who have succeeded them. She did not question the performance, for her own son was the witness testifying through the servant; but she strove to comprehend the power by which work so astonishing could be done by a man. Well enough to make inquiry as to the fact; to comprehend the power, on the other hand, it is first necessary to comprehend God; and he who waits for that will die waiting. With her, however, the hesitation was brief. To Tirzah she said, "This must be the Messiah!"

She spoke not coldly, like one reasoning a doubt away, but as a woman of Israel familiar with the promises of God to her race—a woman of understanding, ready to be glad over the least sign of the realization of the promises.

"There was a time when Jerusalem and all Judea were filled with a story that he was born. I remember it. By this time he should be a man. It must be—it is he. Yes," she said to Amrah, "we will go with you. Bring the water which you will find in the tomb in a jar, and set the food for us. We will eat and be gone."

The breakfast, partaken under excitement, was soon dispatched, and the three women set out on their extraordinary journey. As Tirzah had caught the confident spirit of the others, there was but one fear that troubled the party. Bethany, Amrah said, was the town the man was coming from; now from that to Jerusalem there were three roads, or rather paths—one over the first summit of Olivet, a second at its base, a third between the second summit and the Mount of Offence. The three were not far apart; far enough, however, to make it possible for the unfortunates to miss the Nazarene if they failed the one he chose to come by.

A little questioning satisfied the mother that Amrah knew nothing of the country beyond the Cedron, and even less of the intentions of the man they were going to see, if they could. She discerned, also, that both Amrah and Tirzah—the one from confirmed habits of servitude, the other from natural dependency—looked to her for guidance; and she accepted the charge.

"We will go first to Bethphage," she said to them. "There, if the Lord favor us, we may learn what else to do."

They descended the hill to Tophet and the King's Garden, and paused in the deep trail furrowed through them by centuries of wayfaring.

"I am afraid of the road," the matron said. "Better that we keep to the country among the rocks and trees. This is feast-day, and on the hill-sides yonder I see signs of a great multitude in attendance. By going across the Mount of Offence here we may avoid them."

Tirzah had been walking with great difficulty; upon hearing this her heart began to fail her.

"The mount is steep, Mother; I cannot climb it."

"Remember, we are going to find health and life. See, my child, how the day brightens around us! And yonder are women coming this way to the well. They will stone us if we stay here. Come, be strong this once."

Thus the mother, not less tortured herself, sought to inspire the daughter; and Amrah came to her aid. To this time the latter had not touched the persons of the afflicted, nor they her; now, in disregard of consequences as well as of command, the faithful creature went to Tirzah, and put her arm over her shoulder, and whispered, "Lean on me. I am strong, though I am old; and it is but a little way off. There—now we can go."

The face of the hill they essayed to cross was somewhat broken with pits, and ruins of old structures; but when at last they stood upon the top to rest, and looked at the spectacle presented them over in the northwest—at the Temple and its courtly terraces, at Zion, at the enduring towers white beetling into the sky beyond—the mother was strengthened with a love of life for life's sake.

"Look, Tirzah," she said—"look at the plates of gold on the Gate Beautiful. How they give back the flames of the sun, brightness for brightness! Do you remember we used to go up there? Will it not be pleasant to do so again? And think—home is but a little way off. I can almost see it over the roof of the Holy of Holies; and Judah will be there to receive us!"

From the side of the middle summit garnished green with myrtle and olive trees, they saw, upon looking that way next, thin columns of smoke rising lightly and straight up into the pulseless morning, each a warning of restless pilgrims astir, and of the flight of the pitiless hours, and the need of haste.

Though the good servant toiled faithfully to lighten the labor in descending the hill-side, not sparing herself in the least, the girl moaned at every step; sometimes in extremity of anguish she cried out. Upon reaching the road—that is, the road between the Mount of Offence and the middle or second summit of Olivet—she fell down exhausted.

"Go on with Amrah, mother, and leave me here," she said, faintly.

"No, no, Tirzah. What would the gain be to me if I were healed and you not? When Judah asks for you, as he will, what would I have to say to him were I to leave you?"

"Tell him I loved him."

The elder leper arose from bending over the fainting sufferer, and gazed about her with that sensation of hope perishing which is more nearly like annihilation of the soul than anything else. The supremest joy of the thought of cure was inseparable from Tirzah, who was not too old to forget, in the happiness of healthful life to come, the years of misery by which she had been so reduced in body and broken in spirit. Even as the brave woman was about leaving the venture they were engaged in to the determination of God, she saw a man on foot coming rapidly up the road from the east.

"Courage, Tirzah! Be of cheer," she said. "Yonder I know is one to tell us of the Nazarene."

Amrah helped the girl to a sitting posture, and supported her while the man advanced.

"In your goodness, Mother, you forget what we are. The stranger will go around us; his best gift to us will be a curse, if not a stone."

"We will see."

There was no other answer to be given, since the mother was too well and sadly acquainted with the treatment outcasts of the class to which she belonged were accustomed to at the hands of her countrymen.

As has been said, the road at the edge of which the group was posted was little more than a worn path or trail, winding crookedly through tumult of limestone. If the stranger kept it, he must meet them face to face; and he did so, until near enough to hear the cry she was bound to give. Then, uncovering her head, a further demand of the law, she shouted shrilly,

"Unclean, unclean!"

To her surprise, the man came steadily on.

"What would you have?" he asked, stopping opposite them not four yards off.

"Thou seest us. Have a care," the mother said, with dignity.

"Woman, I am the courier of him who speaketh but once to such as thou and they are healed. I am not afraid."

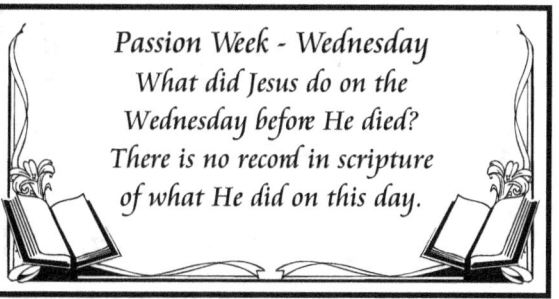

"The Nazarene?"

"The Messiah," he said.

"Is it true that he cometh to the city today?"

"He is now at Bethphage."

"On what road, master?"

"This one."

She clasped her hands, and looked up thankfully.

"For whom takest thou him?" the man asked, with pity.

"The Son of God," she replied.

"Stay thou here then; or, as there is a multitude with him, take thy stand by the rock yonder, the white one under the tree; and as he goeth by fail not to call to him; call, and fear not. If thy faith but equal thy knowledge, he will hear thee though all the heavens thunder. I go to tell Israel, assembled in and about the city, that he is at hand, and to make ready to receive him. Peace to thee and thine, woman."

The stranger moved on.

"Did you hear, Tirzah? Did you hear? The Nazarene is on the road, on this one, and he will hear us. Once more, my child—oh, only once! And let us to the rock. It is but a step."

Thus encouraged Tirzah took Amrah's hand and arose; but as they were going, Amrah said, "Stay; the man is returning." And they waited for him.

"I pray your grace, woman," he said, upon overtaking them. "Remembering that the sun will be hot before the Nazarene arrives, and that the city is near by to give me refreshment should I need it, I thought this water would do thee better than it will me. Take it and be of good cheer. Call to him as he passes."

He followed the words by offering her a gourd full of water, such as foot-travelers sometimes carried with them in their journeys across the hills; and instead of placing the gift on the ground for her to take up when he was at a safe distance, he gave it into her hand.

"Art thou a Jew?" she asked, surprised.

"I am that, and better; I am a disciple of the Christ who teacheth daily by word and example this thing which I have done unto you. The world hath long known the word charity without understanding it. Again I say peace and good cheer to thee and thine."

He went on, and they went slowly to the rock he had pointed out to them, high as their heads, and scarcely thirty yards from the road on the right. Standing in front of it, the mother satisfied herself they could be seen and heard plainly by passers-by whose notice they desired to attract. There they cast themselves under the tree in its shade, and drank of the gourd, and rested refreshed. Ere long Tirzah slept, and fearing to disturb her, the others held their peace.

To be continued!

Easter Party

Easter Hat Sale By Ellye Howell Glover

A clever hostess created this unique party given during the Easter season. There were twenty-four guests, and the invitations read something like this:

"You are bidden to a sale of headgear at the residence of Mr. and Mrs. Blank on the eve of Easter Monday. Please send or bring a hat, bonnet, cap or any form of head covering, either trimmed or untrimmed. This will be the great opportunity of a lifetime to obtain an original headpiece."

And such a variety of parcels, bandboxes, bags and parcels as we found when all had assembled in the spacious living room! The host, a jolly, quick-witted man, acted in the capacity of auctioneer. The guests were provided with tiny candy Easter eggs in little silken bags to use for money, and the bidding waxed fast and furious. Those who drew untrimmed hats had to trim them, making their selections from a table piled high with a conglomeration of feathers, flowers, ribbons and velvets. The hats were something wonderful to behold—Quaker bonnets, sunbonnets, baby bonnets, old Derbies, straw sailors, discarded mushrooms, silken hats of vintage 1873, and a lot of strange shapes and styles, so curious that we all exclaimed: "Did we ever wear such things?" The ice cream was molded in the shape of hats and the strawberries were served in pretty baskets fashioned from dolls' straw hats. This was such a merry, informal affair that I am sure many of the readers will enjoy giving just such a party. Be sure to ask thoroughly congenial people, who will enter into the spirit of the thing and respond heartily. A prize might be offered for the most artistically trimmed hat, choosing for the reward one of the many Easter novelties. Charming hats of crepe paper could be made for souvenirs, distributed to all just before refreshments are served.

Hoop Race for Easter By Ellye Howell Glover

A mother of three dear children entertained at an all day Easter party, the guests being seven of the neighborhood children. The invitations were written on egg-shaped cards sealed with a violet, or the dearest Easter chick just coming out of the shell may be found among the seals or stickers. The ages of the guests ranged from five to eight years. A third floor chamber is known as the children's room, and it was prettily decorated with flowers and branches of budding fruit trees which had been placed in water for several days; there was a mass of blossoms on them by Easter.

Ten little hoops were prepared thus, for one of the games, each one was wound smoothly with a colored tape. The boy who could roll his hoop twice around the room without letting it turnover was awarded a bag of marbles, and the little girl who accomplished the same feat had a dear little doll dressed all in white. A substantial luncheon was served at noon with just the prettiest table imaginable, all glorious jonquils, bunnies, and fluffy yellow chicks. A music box played during the repast. After luncheon the children decorated eggs to take home; and then the last game was best of all. On a white cloth was pasted the head of a beautiful child; the children were blindfolded and told to pin a paper flower on the head of the child. A prize was given for the one who best placed the flower.

Thursday of Passion Week

The Healer
By Lew Wallace
From Ben-Hur, book eighth, chapter IV

During the third hour the road in front of the resting-place of the lepers became gradually more and more frequented by people going in the direction of Bethphage and Bethany; now, however, about the commencement of the fourth hour, a great crowd appeared over the crest of Olivet, and as it defiled down the road thousands in number, the two watchers noticed with wonder that every one in it carried a palm-branch freshly cut. As they sat absorbed by the novelty, the noise of another multitude approaching from the east drew their eyes that way. Then the mother awoke Tirzah.

"What is the meaning of it all?" the latter asked.

"He is coming," answered the mother. "These we see are from the city going to meet him; those we hear in the east are his friends bearing him company; and it will not be strange if the processions meet here before us.

"I fear, if they do, we cannot be heard."

The same thought was in the elder's mind.

"Amrah," she asked, "when Judah spoke of the healing of the ten, in what words did he say they called to the Nazarene?"

"Either they said, 'Lord, have mercy upon us,' or 'Master, have mercy.'"

"Only that?"

"No more that I heard."

"Yet it was enough," the mother added, to herself.

"Yes," said Amrah, "Judah said he saw them go away well."

Meantime the people in the east came up slowly. When at length the foremost of them were in sight, the gaze of the lepers fixed upon a man riding in the midst of what seemed a chosen company which sang and danced about him in extravagance of joy. The rider was bareheaded and clad all in white. When he was in distance to be more clearly observed, these, looking anxiously, saw an olive-hued face shaded by long chestnut hair slightly sunburned and parted in the middle. He looked neither to the right nor left. In the noisy abandon of his followers he appeared to have no part; nor did their favor disturb him in the least, or raise him out of the profound melancholy into which, as his countenance showed, he was plunged. The sun beat upon the back of his head, and lighting up the floating hair gave it a delicate likeness to a golden nimbus. Behind him the irregular procession, pouring forward with continuous singing and shouting, extended out of view. There was no need of any one to tell the lepers that this was he—the wonderful Nazarene!

"He is here, Tirzah," the mother said; "he is here. Come, my child."

As she spoke she glided in front of the white rock and fell upon her knees.

Directly the daughter and servant were by her side. Then at sight of the procession in the west, the thousands from the city halted, and began to wave their green branches, shouting, or rather chanting (for it was all in one voice),

"Blessed is the King of Israel that cometh in the name of the Lord!"

And all the thousands who were of the rider's company, both those near and those afar, replied so the air shook with the sound, which was as a great wind threshing the side of the hill. Amidst the din, the cries of the poor lepers were not more than the twittering of dazed sparrows.

The moment of the meeting of the hosts was come, and with it the opportunity the sufferers were seeking; if not taken, it would be lost forever, and they would be lost as well.

"Nearer, my child—let us get nearer. He cannot hear us," said the mother.

She arose, and staggered forward. Her ghastly hands were up, and she screamed with horrible shrillness. The people saw her—saw her hideous face, and stopped awe-struck—an effect for which extreme human misery, visible as in this instance, is as potent as majesty in purple and gold. Tirzah, behind her a little way, fell down too faint and frightened to follow farther.

"The lepers! The lepers!"

"Stone them!"

"The accursed of God! Kill them!"

These, with other yells of like import, broke in upon the hosannas of the part of the multitude too far removed to see and understand the cause of the interruption. Some there were, however, nearby familiar with the nature of the man to whom the unfortunates were appealing—some who, by long intercourse with him, had caught somewhat of his divine compassion: they gazed at him, and were silent while, in fair view, he rode up and stopped in front of the woman. She also beheld his face—calm, pitiful, and of exceeding beauty, the large eyes tender with benignant purpose.

And this was the colloquy that ensued:

"O Master, Master! Thou seest our need; thou canst make us clean. Have mercy upon us—mercy!"

"Believest thou I am able to do this?" he asked.

"Thou art he of whom the prophets spake—thou art the Messiah!" she replied.

His eyes grew radiant, his manner confident.

"Woman," he said, "great is thy faith; be it unto thee even as thou wilt."

He lingered an instant after, apparently unconscious of the presence of the throng—an instant—then he rode away.

To the heart divinely original, yet so human in all the better elements of humanity, going with sure prevision to a death of all the inventions of men the foulest and most cruel, breathing even then in the forecast shadow of the awful event, and still as hungry and thirsty for love and faith as in the beginning, how precious and ineffably soothing the farewell exclamation of the grateful woman:

"To God in the highest, glory! Blessed, thrice blessed, the Son whom he hath given us!"

Immediately both the hosts, that from the city and that from Bethphage, closed around him with their joyous demonstrations, with hosannas and waving of palms, and so he passed from the lepers forever. Covering her head, the elder hastened to Tirzah, and folded her in her arms, crying, "Daughter, look up! I have his promise; he is indeed the Messiah. We are saved—saved!" And the two remained kneeling while the procession, slowly going, disappeared over the mount. When the noise of its singing afar was a sound scarcely heard the miracle began.

There was first in the hearts of the lepers a freshening of the blood; then it flowed faster and stronger, thrilling their wasted bodies with an infinitely sweet sense of painless healing. Each felt the scourge going from her; their strength revived; they were returning to be themselves. Directly, as if to make the purification complete, from body to spirit the quickening ran, exalting them to a very fervor of ecstasy. The power possessing them to this good end was most nearly that of a draught of swift and happy effect; yet it was unlike and superior in that its healing and cleansing were absolute, and not merely a delicious consciousness while in progress, but the planting, growing, and maturing all at once of a recollection so singular and so holy that the simple thought of it should be of itself ever after a formless yet perfect thanksgiving.

To this transformation—for such it may be called quite as properly as a cure—there was a witness other than Amrah. The reader will remember the constancy with which Ben-Hur had followed the Nazarene throughout his wanderings; and now, recalling the conversation of the night before, there will be little surprise at learning that the young Jew was present when the leprous woman appeared in the path of the pilgrims. He heard her prayer, and saw her disfigured face; he heard the answer also, and was not so accustomed to incidents of the kind, frequent as they had been, as to have lost interest in them. Had such a thing been possible with him, still the bitter disputation always excited by the simplest display of the Master's curative gift would have sufficed to keep his curiosity alive. Besides that, if not above it as an incentive, his hope to satisfy himself upon the vexed question of the mission of the mysterious man was still upon him strong as in the beginning; we might indeed say even stronger, because of a belief that now quickly, before the sun went down, the man himself would make all known by public proclamation. At the close of the scene, consequently, Ben-Hur had withdrawn from the procession, and seated himself upon a stone to wait its passage.

From his place he nodded recognition to many of the people—Galileans in his league, carrying short swords under their long abbas. After a little a swarthy Arab came up leading two horses; at a sign from Ben-Hur he also drew out.

"Stay here," the young master said, when all were gone by, even the laggards. "I wish to be at the city early, and Aldebaran must do me service."

He stroked the broad forehead of the horse, now in his prime of strength and beauty, then crossed the road towards the two women.

They were to him, it should be borne in mind, strangers in whom he felt interest only as they were subjects of a superhuman experiment, the result of which might possibly help him to solution of the mystery that had so long engaged him. As he proceeded, he glanced casually at the figure of the little woman over by the white rock, standing there, her face hidden in her hands.

"As the Lord liveth, it is Amrah!" he said to himself.

He hurried on, and passing by the mother and daughter, still without recognizing them, he stopped before the servant.

"Amrah," he said to her, "Amrah, what do you here?"

She rushed forward, and fell upon her knees before him, blinded by her tears, nigh speechless with contending joy and fear.

"O master, master! Thy God and mine, how good he is!"

The knowledge we gain from much sympathy with others passing through trials is but vaguely understood; strangely enough, it enables us, among other things, to merge our identity into theirs often so completely that their sorrows and their delights become our own. So poor Amrah, aloof and hiding her face, knew the transformation the lepers were undergoing without a word spoken to her—knew it, and shared all their feeling to the full. Her countenance, her words, her whole manner, betrayed her condition; and with swift presentiment he connected it with the women he had just passed: he felt her presence there at that time was in some way associated with them, and turned hastily as they arose to their feet. His heart stood still, he became rooted in his tracks—dumb past outcry—awe-struck.

The woman he had seen before the Nazarene was standing with her hands clasped and eyes streaming, looking towards heaven. The mere transformation would have been a sufficient surprise; but it was the least of the causes of his emotion. Could he be mistaken? Never was there in life a stranger so like his mother; and like her as she was the day the Roman snatched her from him. There was but one difference to mar the identity—the hair of this person was a little streaked with gray; yet that was not impossible of reconcilement, since the intelligence which had directed the miracle might have taken into consideration the natural effects of the passage of years. And who was it by her side, if not Tirzah?—Fair, beautiful, perfect, more mature, but in all other respects exactly the same in appearance as when she looked with him over the parapet the morning of the accident to Gratus. He had given them over as dead, and time had accustomed him to the bereavement; he had not ceased mourning for them, yet, as something distinguishable, they had simply dropped out of his plans and dreams. Scarcely believing his senses, he laid his hand upon the servant's head, and asked, tremulously, "Amrah, Amrah—my mother! Tirzah! Tell me if I see aright."

"Speak to them, O master, speak to them!" she said.

He waited no longer, but ran, with outstretched arms, crying, "Mother! Mother! Tirzah! Here I am!"

They heard his call, and with a cry as loving started to meet him. Suddenly the mother stopped, drew back, and uttered the old alarm,

"Stay, Judah, my son; come not nearer. Unclean, unclean!"

The utterance was not from habit, grown since the dread disease struck her, as much as fear; and the fear was but another form of the ever-thoughtful maternal love. Though they were healed in person, the taint of the scourge might be in their garments ready for communication. He had no such thought. They were before him; he had called them, they had answered. Who or what should keep them from him now? Next moment the three, so long separated, were mingling their tears in each other's arms.

The first ecstasy over, the mother said, "In this happiness, O my children, let us not be ungrateful. Let us begin life anew by acknowledgment of him to whom we are all so indebted."

They fell upon their knees, Amrah with the rest; and the prayer of the elder outspoken was as a psalm.

Tirzah repeated it word for word; so did Ben-Hur, but not with the same clear mind and questionless faith; for when they were risen, he asked,

"In Nazareth, where the man was born, mother, they call him the son of a carpenter. What is he?"

Her eyes rested upon him with all their old tenderness, and she answered as she had answered the Nazarene himself—

"He is the Messiah."

"And whence has he his power?"

"We may know by the use he makes of it. Can you tell me any ill he has done?"

"No."

"By that sign then I answer, He has his power from God."

It is not an easy thing to shake off in a moment the expectations nurtured through years until they have become essentially a part of us; and though Ben-Hur asked himself what the vanities of the world were to such a one, his ambition was obdurate and would not down. He persisted as men do yet every day in measuring the Christ by himself. How much better if we measured ourselves by the Christ!

Naturally, the mother was the first to think of the cares of life.

"What shall we do now, my son? Where shall we go?"

Then Ben-Hur, recalled to duty, observed how completely every trace of the scourge had disappeared from his restored people; that each had back her perfection of person; that, as with Naaman when he came up out of the water, their flesh had come again like unto the flesh of a little child; and he took off his cloak, and threw it over Tirzah.

"Take it," he said, smiling; "the eye of the stranger would have shunned you before, now it shall not offend you."

The act exposed a sword belted to his side.

"Is it a time of war?" asked the mother, anxiously.

"No."

"Why, then, are you armed?"

"It may be necessary to defend the Nazarene."

Thus Ben-Hur evaded the whole truth.

"Has he enemies? Who are they?"

"Alas, Mother, they are not all Romans!"

"Is he not of Israel, and a man of peace?"

"There was never one more so; but in the opinion of the rabbis and teachers he is guilty of a great crime."

"What crime?"

"In his eyes the uncircumcised Gentile is as worthy favor as a Jew of the strictest habit. He preaches a new dispensation."

The mother was silent, and they moved to the shade of the tree by the rock. Calming his impatience to have them home again and hear their story, he showed them the necessity of obedience to the law governing in cases like theirs, and in conclusion called the Arab, bidding him take the horses to the gate by Bethesda and await him there;

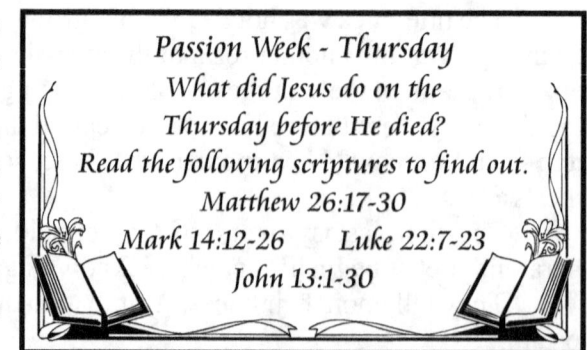

Passion Week - Thursday
What did Jesus do on the Thursday before He died?
Read the following scriptures to find out.
Matthew 26:17-30
Mark 14:12-26   Luke 22:7-23
John 13:1-30

whereupon they set out by the way of the Mount of Offence. The return was very different from the coming; they walked rapidly and with ease, and in good time reached a tomb newly made near that of Absalom, overlooking the depths of Cedron. Finding it unoccupied, the women took possession, while he went on hastily to make the preparations required for their new condition.

Easter Songs

Sing the two songs together as a family. Discuss what the songs mean. If you are not familiar with these songs, sing some Easter songs that you know (look in a hymnal for ideas).

When I Survey the Wondrous Cross

Isaac Watts, 1707

Gregorian Chant
Arranged by Lowell Mason, 1824

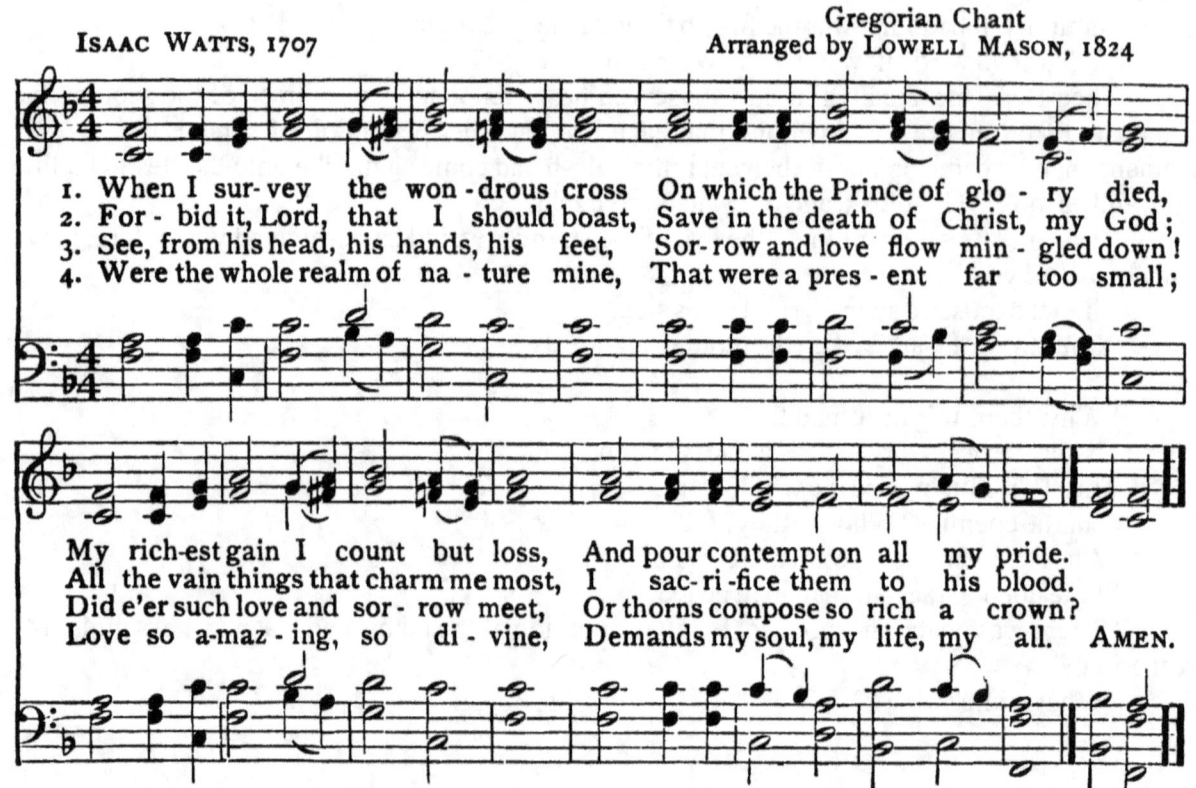

1. When I survey the wondrous cross On which the Prince of glory died, My richest gain I count but loss, And pour contempt on all my pride.
2. Forbid it, Lord, that I should boast, Save in the death of Christ, my God; All the vain things that charm me most, I sacrifice them to his blood.
3. See, from his head, his hands, his feet, Sorrow and love flow mingled down! Did e'er such love and sorrow meet, Or thorns compose so rich a crown?
4. Were the whole realm of nature mine, That were a present far too small; Love so amazing, so divine, Demands my soul, my life, my all. AMEN.

Countdown to Easter

Passover
Good Friday

Miss Rebecca's Easter Blossoms
By Harriet A. Nash

*I*t was only a boy standing on the highest step and reaching for the great brass knocker of Miss Rebecca Grant's side door: a thin-haired, freckle-faced boy, with no feature to distinguish him from a hundred other boys. Whether the torn hat and ragged jacket covered the possibilities of future statesmanship, or the grimy little fingers might someday grasp with power the pen or sword, not even the closest observer could have guessed. To Miss Rebecca, as she opened the door the fraction of an inch, the little figure was closely suggestive of the one class of males which her soul abhorred.

"I never feed tramps," she announced in a crushing tone, before her caller could speak. The boy ignored her announcement.

"Please, miss," he asked with dignity, "do you want a hired man?"

The saving grace of Miss Rebecca's proud nature was a sense of humor. A grim smile hovered about her thin lips as she looked critically down upon the morsel of humanity. A sudden recognition chased away the smile. "You belong at the poor farm," she said severely. "I saw you there last week."

"Yes'm," assented the boy. "I saw you. You said the farm was a safe and proper refuge for the old and helpless, but a livin' disgrace to the able bodied. Please 'm I'm able bodied. I can bring water and wash dishes and clean knives. And I ain't afraid of anything, even in the dark."

Miss Rebecca knew she should have sent the child straight back to the poor farm. But instead it came to pass that two hours later Jimmie Snow sat eating his first self-earned supper from the oilcloth cover of her kitchen table. Through the open door of the dining room, where Miss Grant in solitary state maintained all the elegance due her name and position, he caught glimpses of bright carpet and mahogany sideboard, of snowy cloth and shining silver. Beyond the dining room there opened a marvelous vista of easy-chairs and pictures and a bay window full of blossoming plants. Jimmie drew a deep breath of delight as he gazed across the two rooms upon the glowing colors of a scarlet geranium. Flowers in summer might be had for the seeking, and from the time the first pink buds of the mayflower nestled in his little moist palm to the last wind-beaten blossoms of the frost flower, they were his daily delight. But flowers in winter—he had never been so near to them before.

He sat alone by the kitchen fire, while Miss Rebecca went forth to attend the mid-week prayer meeting, and groped sleepily up the back stairs, when, on her return, she directed him to the tiny kitchen chamber. "When I'm a man," he murmured drowsily to himself as he sank into boyish slumber, "I'm goin' to have a big square house, with flowers in every window; and eat off of a white table, with lots of shiny dishes."

The neighbors called it charity on Miss Rebecca's part. Miss Rebecca herself called it a whim, and being a woman little given to whims, atoned to herself for the weakness by an added dignity in her manner towards her new employee. But Jimmie, whose philosophical little mind had early learned to rely upon its own conclusions, knew that he was no longer a town pauper, but had now become a self-supporting citizen. He had not been unhappy at the poor farm. As he sat alone at Miss Rebecca's kitchen table, it may be that he thought regretfully of the lively chatter at the long table, or on winter evenings missed the rambling stories which the old people were wont to tell. But no one knew; even those who know and love them can only guess at the marvelous workings in the mind of a little boy. And in Jimmie's case there was no one who cared to guess.

He went daily to the village school in garments cut over from Judge Grant's by patterns which had been used for Miss Rebecca's brothers. And Miss Rebecca, scorning to waste money on the village barber, cut his hair straight across behind his ears, after a pattern of her own invention. The other boys laughed at first; but after a little, one and another having felt the force of Jimmie's strong little fists, they conceived therefore a respect which outweighed any peculiarities in dress. Out of school there was abundant occupation in filling the kitchen wood box, cleaning knives and running errands. And in the brief periods of play, snow houses must be constructed and interesting toys made from bits of wood, pieces of string and empty spools.

All this time, according to Miss Rebecca's express command, his feet never once trespassed beyond the dining room door. Miss Rebecca would do her duty by her native town, and this its orphan charge. But she had no intention that her neat carpets be defaced by masculine tread or her household treasures displaced by childish fingers.

Early in March, Miss Grant sent Jimmie across the snowy fields with an urgent message. "Tell Freeman Morgan I want that dry wood he was to deliver here in October," she commanded. "I should have known better than to deal with people of such procrastinating tendencies."

Jimmie looked a little shocked. He didn't know what those last two words meant, but Miss Grant's tone signified dreadful possibilities.

Mr. Morgan was full of regrets. "I'll be right around with it next week," he promised. "I've been that drove up all winter, I ain't been able to get to it."

Two weeks later Jimmie went again.

"I'll bring it tomorrow," promised the farmer. "I clean forgot it last week."

But tomorrow and next day came and went, and to Jimmie's dismay the steadily diminishing wood pile was unreplenished. On the third day he came home from school in the late afternoon to find Miss Rebecca in deep distress, her best bonnet on, and an open telegram in her hand. Jimmie wonderingly obeyed her summons to the sitting room.

"I've got to go to the city," announced Miss Rebecca. "There's trouble about those railroad bonds that father would buy, though I told him better." Jimmie wondered just what "railroad bonds" might be but he only said "Yes'm" in a sympathetic tone; which evidently was all that Miss Rebecca expected, for she continued, "I shall leave the care of everything to you, and over 'n' above everything else you're to take care of these plants. The geraniums are all in bloom, and the roses and lilies will be out for Easter next Sunday. I wouldn't have one of 'em freeze for a hundred dollars."

There followed careful directions as to the temperature of the room and watering the plants. "Mind you don't get a drop on the carpet," cautioned Miss Rebecca. "And you better sleep right here on the couch to keep the fire going. I shall stop and send Henry Applebee after that wood."

"Yes'm," said Jimmie.

Miss Rebecca looked wistfully about her. The room was cozy and warm, but a cloudy twilight was settling over the gloomy world outside. For nine years she had not spent a night away from home. A thrill of homesickness softened her voice as she said, "I'm sure I can trust you, James. You've been a good boy and never told me an untruth. There's plenty of food on the pantry shelf, and I sh'll be home tomorrow night. You must stay at home and keep the fire. Henry will bring the wood tomorrow."

"Yes'm," said Jimmie, his heart swelling with delight in her commendation. "I knew I was able bodied," he declared exultantly to himself.

Miss Rebecca called back to him from the front doorstep. "Mind you don't let those plants freeze," she said with emphasis, "if you have to burn Grandfather Grant's sideboard to keep a fire." After she was gone, Jimmie ate his supper and brought in all the wood that remained in the pile. It was dark by this time and his eyes turned questioningly towards the row of shining lamps on the kitchen shelf. But Miss Rebecca had never permitted him to light a lamp, and her recent instructions had failed to touch upon the question.

"I c'n get along," said Jimmie sturdily, as he groped his way back to the sitting room.

Twice in the night, oppressed by a sense of responsibility, he awoke to look carefully after the fire. It was not lonely, for the tall clock in the corner ticked pleasantly, and though he could not see them, he knew there were the flowers and pictures to keep him company. At the second waking he heard the wind whistling drearily about the great house and icy snowflakes beating upon the window panes. Morning found the fields, which had been bare and brown the night before, deeply covered with snow, which the wind was tossing about at will. "It's the line gale and a blizzard both to once," decided Jimmie in boyish delight. But his face grew serious as he looked out through the swiftly falling flakes at the drifting highway.

"I'm afraid Henry Applebee'll be bothered about the wood," he said anxiously. Fire in the kitchen was not to be thought of. Jimmie ate his breakfast in the chilly pantry, blowing upon his fingers to keep them warm, and carefully picking up all the crumbs. Then having watered the plants with loving care, he looked about him for occupation. There were many books upon the shelves—books which must be full of pictures, and Jimmie loved pictures next to flowers. Miss Rebecca had not said he might look at them, but something within him seemed to whisper that she would never know. But with his eyes on a large green and gold volume, he paused and the outstretched hand fell to his side.

"She said she could trust me," he said slowly. "She didn't mean just able bodied only, but able minded too. I won't touch them."

He went out to the wood shed and looked longingly at the little pile of self-made toys. He had sometimes been allowed to have them in the kitchen on snowy days, but the sitting room? No, it would never do. However, Jimmie was by no means at the end of his resources. And presently he was settled on the rug before the fire, with his own school geography. Not to study; oh, no. But the colored maps afforded an enticing occupation in tracing long journeys which he meant to take in that future of boundless promise—"when I grow up!"

The drift grew higher. Henry Applebee and the wood came not. Neither when night fell did Miss Rebecca return, for the little branch railroad which once each day ran a train into Plainville Centre was now impassable.

"Tomorrow I'll go over to Mr. Moon's and borrow some wood," decided Jimmie as he stood in the gathering darkness by the window, and strained his eyes to catch, through the storm, a glimmer of light from Miss Grant's nearest neighbor, a full quarter mile away.

When morning came he placed the last stick of wood upon the fire, and started forth, not unpleased at the necessity of facing the storm. But the snow was deep and the wind fierce. Again and again a baffled little figure crept back to the sheltered doorway, to regain its breath. At the last attempt he struggled for a long time in a huge drift by the gate, and only by great effort regained the steps once more. "I ain't so very able bodied after all," gasped Jimmie as he brushed the clinging snow from his garments.

The last stick of wood had burned to coals. With sober face Jimmie brought in from the wood shed his cherished playthings, and placed them one by one upon the fire. A little cart, made from a salt box with spools for wheels, went last of all. These lasted an hour. His schoolbooks came next. Then he made another trip to the wood shed and came back with axe and saw. "I should have used the kitchen chairs and table first," he remarked to himself. "But she said the sideboard." With great effort he pushed the cumbrous piece of furniture into the kitchen—there must be no sawdust or splinters on the dining room carpet—and five minutes later the slender arms of Miss Rebecca's "hired man" were bravely attacking the inlaid sideboard which had come across the ocean with the earliest Grants and had been the pride of each succeeding owner's heart.

It was Saturday before the wind subsided and the welcome sight of "breaking out" teams was seen upon the streets of Plainville. And late that afternoon the first train from the city puffed wearily into the little station. Miss Rebecca stepped from the long covered "depot pung" to her own well brushed doorsteps, just as Henry Applebee drove up with a load of wood. In stony silence she received Henry's apologies, not daring to glance up at the sitting room windows, where limp and lifeless must stand her beloved plants.

All traces of disaster had vanished from the kitchen floor, but in the chilly dining room Miss Rebecca paused, her eyes fixed upon the empty corner. With a sudden thrill of horror she recalled her last reckless command to Jimmie. Was the boy an idiot?

Anger, grief, and desolated family pride possessed her as she opened the sitting room door.

The room was warm: and a fragrance as if from summer gardens filled the air. Between her and the window stood Jimmie, his whole face shining with rapture. "Look!" he cried.

Behind him was a mass of bloom. Above the geraniums roses white and crimson hung heavy upon their stems, and from the glossy leaves of the lily rose seven pure blossoms with hearts of gold.

> Passion Week - Good Friday
> What did Jesus do on Good Friday?
> Read the following scriptures to find out.
> Matthew 27:1-66
> Mark 15:1-47   Luke 22:66-23:56
> John 18:28-19:37

Miss Rebecca drew a deep breath and looked downward to where the last broken pieces of Grandfather Grant's sideboard lay in the wood basket. "I had to burn it just as you told me," Jimmie explained cheerfully. "But of course you wouldn't give the lily for a thousand sideboards." Was it the fragrance of her home coming, the Easter message of the lily or the boy's rapt face? Within Miss Rebecca's breast there stirred to life that mother-love without which no true woman's heart was ever given her from God. The hard crust, which years of loneliness and pride had formed, melted before it.

What, after all, were the cherished possessions of dead and gone Grants in comparison with this eager human life, full of wondrous possibilities of goodness and greatness? What were perishable blossoms to the light shining through those clear blue eyes, straight out from the immortal soul of a ten-year-old boy?

"You blessed little creature!" she said with her arms around the child. "Your faithful little heart is worth more than all the old furniture that ever came across the seas. You're going to be my own little boy from this minute."

Jimmie submitted to the caress; it was not unpleasant since there were no other boys present.

"And sit in this room evenings—with you—and the flowers?" he asked. He walked to church through the melting snow next morning, his hand clasped in Miss Rebecca's and a red rose pinned upon his Sunday jacket; and came home to eat his Easter dinner, sitting opposite her at the round table, and drinking from a silver cup, a full century older than himself.

"He setteth the solitary in families" murmured Miss Rebecca, in place of her usual grace. "To think it's taken me all these weeks to learn that 'twas meant for us two solitaries to unite and make a family." Jimmie looked at her thoughtfully. The journey and anxiety of the past week had left traces of weariness upon her face.

"When I'm a man," he said to himself, "I shall take care of the wood and 'railroad bonds' and everything else that bothers her." But all he said aloud was, "Yes'm."

LEGEND OF THE NAILS

An old legend says that the nails used to crucify Jesus were forged by a Gypsy smith and that this had accounted for much of the persecution the Gypsy's had endured throughout the ages. By another legend a Gypsy woman, passing by as they were about to crucify Jesus, whipped up one of the nails they were going to use. She would fain have stolen all four, but could not. Her theft is the cause why one nail only was used for the two feet. In truth it matters not who made the nails that held Jesus to the Cross because it was actually our sins that bound Him to the Cross.

Easter Cooking

Hot Cross Buns

1 cup milk
¼ cup water
¼ cup sugar
2 Tbls. shortening or butter
3 cups flour
   (add an additional ¼ cup flour if needed)
½ tsp. salt
1 tsp. cinnamon
1 package of yeast or 2 tsp. active dry yeast
1 egg well beaten
½ cup currants (raisins may be substituted)

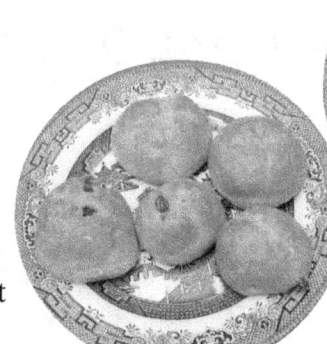

Above - Baked and frosted
Left - Baked

Warm milk, shortening, and water to about 120° F. Add sugar to the warm milk and stir to mix. While milk is warming, combine flour, salt, cinnamon, and yeast; mix well. Add the warmed milk mixture to the flour and mix well, then add the well beaten egg. Dough will be soft. Add dried currants or raisins. Cover with a damp cloth and let rise until double, about 1 hour.

Shape into moderate sized biscuits and place one inch apart on a greased cookie sheet. Using a sharp knife, score a cross in the top of each bun. Brush the tops with part of a well beaten egg. Let rise to double their bulk. Bake 20 minutes at 350° F. When cool make a cross of icing on the top of each.

Frosting
Mix together 1¾ cup confectioners sugar, ½ tsp. vanilla, and 2 Tbls. hot water. Put frosting in a sandwich bag and seal tightly. Snip a corner of the bag and squeeze the frosting through the hole. Make a cross of icing on the top of each.

History of Hot Cross Buns
By William Tegg

This custom is said to have originated from the fast of Good Friday, but it is also in remembrance of the apostolic custom of breaking bread from house to house. It is likely that buns or cakes, something similar to those in use at present, were employed in this manner in the early ages of Christianity. It is to be observed also, that if four persons divide a bun among them, each taking a division, they will naturally stand in the form of a cross, and the bun will break at its partitions. Thus, both the position of the parties, and the figure in which the bun breaks, as well as the act of breaking, are emblematical of the crucifixion.

Hot Cross Buns!

Hot cross buns!
Hot cross buns!
One a penny, two a penny,
Hot cross buns!

Hot cross buns!
Hot cross buns!
If you have no daughters,
Give them to your sons!

And if you have neither,
Then eat them all yourselves!

Saturday Before Easter

The General's Easter Box
By Temple Bailey

*T*he General did not look at all as one would expect a general to look. He was short and thickset and had a red face and a white mustache, and he usually dressed in a gray tweed suit, with a funny Norfolk jacket with a belt, and wore a soft cap pulled down almost to his eyeglasses.

And he always did his own marketing. That is how he came to know Jimmy.

Jimmy stood at a corner of Old Market and sold little bundles of dried sage and sweet marjoram, and sassafras and cinnamon, and soup-bunches made of bits of vegetables tied together—a bit of parsley and a bit of celery and a bit of carrot and a sprig of summer savory, all for one cent. Then at Christmas-time he displayed wreaths, which he and his little mother made at home, and as the spring came on he brought wild flowers that he picked in the woods.

And that was how he came to know the General.

For one morning, just before Easter, the General came puffing down the outside aisle of Old Market, with his servant man behind him with an enormous basket. The General's carriage was drawn up to the curbstone, and the gray horses were dancing little fancy dances over the asphalt street, when all at once Jimmy thrust a bunch of arbutus under the General's very nose.

"Go away, go away!" said the General, and trotted down to the carriage door, which a footman held open for him.

But a whiff of fragrance had reached him, and he stopped.

"How much?" he asked.

"Three cents," said Jimmy, in a hoarse voice.

The General looked at the little fellow through his eye-glasses.

"Got a cold?" he inquired gruffly.

"Yes, sir," croaked Jimmy.

"Why don't you stay in the house, then?" growled the General.

"Can't, sir," said Jimmy, cheerfully; "business is business."

The General looked at the little stand where " business " was transacted—at the little rows of dried stuffs, at the small basket of flowers, and at the soup-bunches.

"Humph," he said.

Then his hand went down into his pocket, and he pulled out a lot of change. After that he chose two bunches of sweet, pinky blossoms.

"Two for five, sir," said Jimmy.

"Hum," said the General. "You might give me some parsley and a soup-bunch."

Jimmy wrapped up the green stuff carefully and dropped it into the basket carried by the servant.

"Nine cents, sir," he said; and the General handed him a dime and then moved to the next stall, holding the flowers close to his nose.

"You forgot your change," cried Jimmy, and rushed after him with the one cent.

"Keep—" But one look at the honest little face and he changed his sentence.

"Thank you, young man," he said, and away he drove.

After that Jimmy looked for the General, and the General for Jimmy. Their transactions were always carried on in a strictly business manner, although, to be sure, the General's modest family of two did not require the unlimited sage and sweet marjoram that were ordered from time to time.

On the Saturday before Easter the little stand was bright with new wares. In little nests of dried grasses lay eggs—Easter eggs, bright pink and blue and purple and mottled. Jimmy had invested in a dozen at forty cents the dozen, and he had hopes of doubling the money, for work surely counted for something, and he and the Little Mother had dyed them.

But somehow people passed them by. Inside of the market there were finer nests, and eggs gilded and lettered, and Jimmy began to feel that his own precious eggs were very dull indeed.

But when the General appeared around the corner, the boy's spirits rose. Here, at any rate, was a good customer.

The General, however, was in a temper. There had been an argument with the fish-man which had left him red in the face and very touchy. So he bought two bunches of arbutus and nothing else.

"Any eggs, sir?" asked Jimmy.

"Eggs?" said the General, looking over the little stand.

"Easter eggs," explained Jimmy.

"I've no use for such things," said the General.

"Oh!" said Jimmy, and in spite of himself his voice trembled. When one is the man of the family, and the Little Mother is sewing for dear life, and her work and the little stand in the market are all that pay the rent and buy food, it is sometimes hard to be brave. But the General did not notice the tremble.

Jimmy tried again: "Any children, sir? Children always like Easter eggs, you know."

"No," said the General; "no one but a son in the Philippines—a son some six feet two in his stockings."

"Any grandchildren, sir?" hopefully.

"Bless my soul," said the General, testily, "what a lot of questions!" And he hurried off to his carriage.

Jimmy felt very forlorn. The General had been his last hope. The eggs were a dead loss.

At last it came time to close up, and he piled all of his wares in a basket. Then he took out a little broom and began to sweep in an orderly way around his little stall. He had a battered old dustpan, and as he carried it out to the street to empty it, he saw a stiff greenish gray paper sticking out of the dirt. Nothing in the world ever looks exactly like that but an American greenback, and, sure enough, when Jimmy pulled it out it proved to be a ten-dollar bill.

Jimmy sat down on the curb suddenly. His money always came in pennies and nickels and dimes and quarters. The Little Mother sometimes earned a dollar at a time, but never in his whole life had Jimmy possessed a ten-dollar bill.

Think of the possibilities to a little, poor, cold, worried boy. There was two months' rent in that ten-dollar bill—two months in which he would not have to worry over whether there would be a roof over their heads.

Then there was a basket stall in that ten-dollar bill. That had always been his ambition. Someone had told him that baskets sold well in other cities, and not a single person had opened a basket stall in Old Market, and that was Jimmy's chance. Once established, he knew he could earn a good living.

As for ten dollars' worth of groceries and provisions, Jimmy's mind could not grasp such a thing; fifty cents had always been the top limit for a grocery bill.

But—it wasn't Jimmy's ten dollars. Like a flash his dreams tumbled to the ground. There had been many people coming and going through Old Market, but Jimmy knew that the bill was the General's. For the old gentleman had pulled out a roll when he reached for the five cents. Yes, it was the General's; but how to find the General?

Inside the market he found the General's butcher. Yes, the butcher knew the General's address, for he was one of his best customers, and would keep Jimmy's basket while the boy went to the house.

It was a long distance. Jimmy passed rows of great stone mansions, and went through parks, where crocuses and hyacinths were just peeping out.

At last he came to the General's. A servant answered the ring of the bell, "Who shall I say?" he inquired loftily, "The General is very busy, y' know."

"Say Jimmy, from the market, please," and Jimmy sat down on the great hall seat, feeling very much awed with all the magnificence.

"Well, well," said the General, as he came puffing down the stairs. "Well, well, and what do you want?"

Please, sir, did you drop this?" and Jimmy held out the tightly rolled bill.

"Did I? Well, now, I'm sure I don't know. Perhaps I did, perhaps I did."

"I found it in front of my stall," said Jimmy.

What a strange thing it seemed that the General should not know! Jimmy would have known if he had lost a penny. He began to feel that the General could not have a true idea of business.

The General took out a roll of bills. "Let me see," he said. "Here's my market list. Yes, I guess that's mine, sure enough."

"I'm glad I noticed it," said Jimmy, simply. "I came near sweeping it into the street."

"And what can I pay you for your trouble?" asked the General, looking at the boy keenly.

"Well," said Jimmy, stoutly, "you see, business is business, and I had to take my time, and I'd like to get back as soon as I can."

The General frowned. He was afraid he was going to be disappointed in this boy. What, after all, if he was a beggar—

"And so," went on Jimmy, "if you would give me a nickel for car-fare, I think we might call it square."

The General fumbled around for his eyeglasses, put them on, and looked at Jimmy in astonishment.

"A nickel?" he asked.

"Yes, sir," Jimmy blushed. "You know, I ought to get back."

"Well, well," said the General. The boy had certainly the instincts of a gentleman. Not a single plea of poverty, and yet one could see that he was poor, very poor.

Just then a gong struck softly somewhere. "I'm not going to let you go until you have a bit of lunch with us," said the General. "I have told my wife of Jimmy of the market, and now I want you to meet her."

So Jimmy went down into a wonderful dining room, where the silver and the cut glass shone, and where at the farther side of the table was the sweetest little old lady, who came and shook hands with him.

Jimmy had never before eaten lunch where the soup was served in little cups, but the General's wife put him at his ease when she told him that his very own soup-bunches were in that soup, and if he didn't eat plenty of it he wouldn't be advertising his wares. Then the General, with knife upraised, stopped in his carving of the cold roast chicken, and turned to Jimmy with a smile of approval in his genial face, and said that it was his sage, too, that was in the chicken dressing.

They made Jimmy talk, and finally he told them of his ambition for a basket stall.

"And when do you expect to get it?" asked the General, with a smile.

"When I get the goose that lays the golden egg, I am afraid, sir," said Jimmy, a little sadly.

Then the General's wife asked questions, and Jimmy told her about the Little Mother, and of their life together; but not one word did he tell of their urgent need, for Jimmy had not learned to beg.

At last the wonderful lunch was over, somewhat to Jimmy's relief, it must be confessed.

"I shall come and see your mother, Jimmy," said the General's wife, as Jimmy left her.

Out in the hall the General handed the boy a nickel. "Business is business, young man," he said, with a twinkle in his eye.

That night Jimmy and his mother sat up very late, for the boy had so much to tell.

"Do you think I was wrong to ask for the nickel, Mother?" he asked anxiously, when he had finished.

"No," said his mother; "but I am glad you didn't ask for more."

Then, after Jimmy had gone to bed, the mother sat up for a long time, wondering how the rent was to be paid.

On Easter Monday morning Jimmy and the Little Mother started out to pick the arbutus and the early violets which Jimmy was to sell Tuesday at his little stall.

It was a sunshiny morning. The broad road was hard and white after the April showers, the sky was blue, and the air was sweet with the breath of bursting buds. And, in spite of cares, Jimmy and his mother had a very happy time as they filled their baskets.

At last they sat down to tie up the bunches. Carriage after carriage passed them. As the last bunch of flowers was laid in Jimmy's basket, a Victoria drawn by a pair of grays stopped in front of the flower-gatherers.

"Well, well," said a hearty voice, and there were the General and his wife! They had called for Jimmy and his mother, they said, and had been directed to the wooded hill.

"Get in, get in," commanded the General; and, in spite of the Little Mother's hesitancy and timid protests, she was helped up beside the General's wife by the footman, while Jimmy hopped in beside the General, and away they went over the hard white road.

The General was in a happy mood.

"Well, my boy, have you found your golden egg?" he asked Jimmy.

"No, sir," said Jimmy, gravely; "not yet."

"Too bad, too bad," said the old gentleman, while he shifted a white box that was on the seat between himself and Jimmy to the other side.

"You're quite sure, are you, that you could only get it from a goose?" he asked later.

"Get what, sir?" said Jimmy, whose eyes were on the cheerful crowds that thronged the sidewalks.

"The egg," said the General.

"Oh—yes, sir," replied Jimmy, with a smile.

The General leaned back and laughed and laughed until he was red in the face; but Jimmy could see nothing to laugh at, so he merely smiled politely, and wondered what the joke was.

At last they reached Jimmy's home, and the General helped the Little Mother out. As he did so he handed her a white box. Jimmy was busy watching the gray horses, and saw nothing else.

"For the boy," whispered the General.

The Little Mother shook her head doubtfully.

"Bless you, madam," cried the General, testily, "I have a boy of my own—if he is six feet two in his stockings." Then, in a softer tone, "I beg of you to take it, madam; it will please an old man and give the boy a start."

So when goodbye had been said, and Jimmy stood looking after the carriage and the prancing grays, the Little Mother put the white box in his hand.

Jimmy opened it, and there on a nest of white cotton was an egg. But it was different from any of the eggs that Jimmy had sold on Saturday. It was large and gilded, and around the middle was a yellow ribbon.

Jimmy lifted it out, and found it very heavy.

"What do you think it is?" he said.

"Untie the ribbon," advised his mother, whose quick eyes saw a faint line which showed an opening.

Jimmy pulled the yellow ribbon, the upper half of the egg opened on a hinge, and there, side by side, were glistening gold coins—five-dollar gold pieces, and five of them.

"Oh!" said Jimmy, and he sat down on the step, breathless with surprise and joy.

A slip of white paper lay between two of the coins. Jimmy snatched it out, and this is what he read:

Please accept the contents of the golden egg, with the best wishes of,
The Goose

And then at last Jimmy saw the joke.

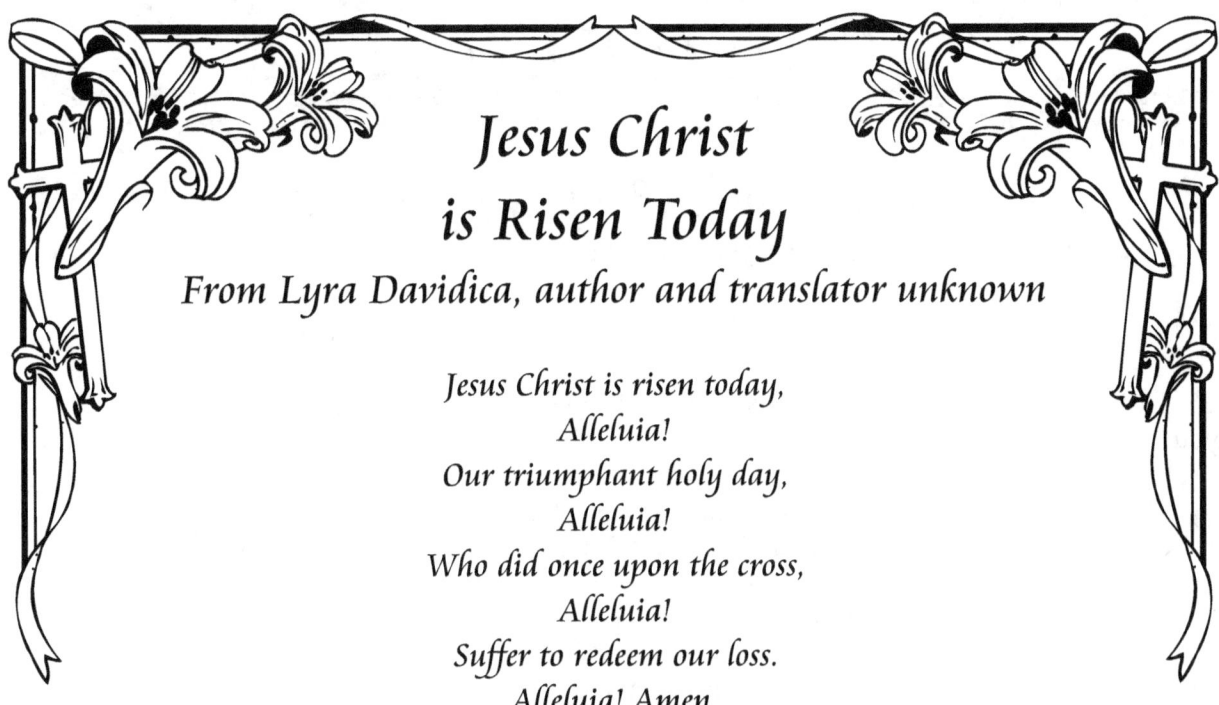

Jesus Christ is Risen Today

From Lyra Davidica, author and translator unknown

Jesus Christ is risen today,
Alleluia!
Our triumphant holy day,
Alleluia!
Who did once upon the cross,
Alleluia!
Suffer to redeem our loss.
Alleluia! Amen.

Hymns of praise then let us sing
Unto Christ, our heavenly King,
Who endured the cross and grave,
Sinners to redeem and save.
Alleluia!

But the pains which He endured,
Our salvation hath procured;
Now above the sky He's King,
Where the angels ever sing
Alleluia!

Sing we to our God above
Praise eternal as His love;
Praise Him, all ye heavenly host,
Father, Son, and Holy Ghost;
Alleluia! Amen.

Easter Quiz

Who Said It? By Amy Puetz

Match the speaker on the right with the quote on the left. Answers are below.

A) "What is truth?"

B) "Even if I have to die with you, I will never disown you."

C) "Have nothing to do with that innocent man, for I have suffered a great deal today in a dream because of him."

D) "Why do you look for the living among the dead?"

E) "Father, forgive them for they know not what they do."

F) "Unless I see the nail marks in his hands and put my finger where the nails were, and put my hand into his side, I will not believe it."

G) "Surly this man was the son of God."

H) "What are you willing to give me if I hand him over to you?"

I) "Rabboni!"

1) Judas

2) Angel

3) Pilate

4) Mary Magdalene

5) Pilate's wife

6) Jesus

7) Thomas

8) Peter

9) Roman solider

Answers: A-3, B-8, C-5, D-2, E-6, F-7, G-9, H-1, I-4

Countdown to Easter — Amy Puetz

Easter - Resurrection Sunday

The Loveliest Rose in the World
By Hans Christian Andersen

Once there reigned a queen, in whose garden were found the most glorious flowers at all seasons and from all the lands of the world. But more than all others she loved the roses, and she had many kinds of this flower, from the wild dog-rose with its apple-scented green leaves to the most splendid, large, crimson roses. They grew against the garden walls, wound themselves around the pillars and wind-frames, and crept through the windows into the rooms, and all along the ceilings in the halls. And the roses were of many colors, and of every fragrance and form.

But care and sorrow dwelt in those halls. The queen lay upon a sick-bed, and the doctors said she must die.

"There is still one thing that can save her," said the wise man. "Bring her the loveliest rose in the world, the rose that is the symbol of the purest, the brightest love. If that is held in front of her eyes before they close, she will not die."

Then old and young came from every side with roses, the loveliest that bloomed in each garden, but they were not of the right sort. The flower was to be plucked from the Garden of Love. But what rose in all that garden expressed the highest and purest love?

And the poets sang of the loveliest rose in the world,—of the love of maid and youth, and of the love of dying heroes.

"But they have not named the right flower," said the wise man. "They have not pointed out the place where it blooms in its splendor. It is not the rose that springs from the hearts of youthful lovers, though this rose will ever be fragrant in song. It is not the bloom that sprouts from the blood flowing from the breast of the hero who dies for his country, though few deaths are sweeter than his, and no rose is redder than the blood that flows then. Nor is it the wondrous flower to which man devotes many a sleepless night and much of his fresh life,—the magic flower of science."

"But I know where it blooms," said a happy mother, who came with her pretty child to the bedside of the dying queen. "I know where the loveliest rose of love may be found. It springs in the blooming cheeks of my sweet child, when, waking from sleep, it opens its eyes and smiles tenderly at me."

"Lovely is this rose, but there is a lovelier still," said the wise man.

"I have seen the loveliest, purest rose that blooms," said a woman. "I saw it on the cheeks of the queen. She had taken off her golden crown. And in the long, dreary night she carried her sick child in her arms. She wept, kissed it, and prayed for her child."

"Holy and wonderful is the white rose of a mother's grief," answered the wise man, "but it is not the one we seek."

"The loveliest rose in the world I saw at the altar of the Lord," said the good Bishop, "the young maidens went to the Lord's Table. Roses were blushing and pale roses shining on their fresh cheeks. A young girl stood there. She looked with all the love and purity of her spirit up to heaven. That was the expression of the highest and purest love."

"May she be blessed," said the wise man, "but not one of you has yet named the loveliest rose in the world."

Then there came into the room a child, the queen's little son.

"Mother," cried the boy, "only hear what I have read."

And the child sat by the bedside and read from the Book of Him who suffered death upon the cross to save men, and even those who were not yet born. "Greater love there is not."

And a rosy glow spread over the cheeks of the queen, and her eyes gleamed, for she saw that from the leaves of the Book there bloomed the loveliest rose, that sprang from the blood of Christ shed on the cross.

"I see it!" she said, "He who beholds this, the loveliest rose on earth, shall never die."

Easter Poem
By Caleb Davis Bradlee

All hail to Easter Day now here;
Away at once our doubt and fear,
For Christ has risen!
Our hearts shall rise in sacred love,
Our eyes shall turn to thee above,
O God of Heaven!

We feel the reign of time has fled,
No longer can the seeming dead
In sleep repose!
The soul will find another home,
And hear the Savior's solemn 'Come,'
When breath shall close!

We know this life will speed away,
And short will be our mortal day,
And flesh must fade!
But still beyond there is a rest
For all the holy and the blest
Who've Christ obeyed!

Thanks be to God for Easter Day,
To Jesus, too, who led the way
To grace and peace!
And may we all receive a crown
When we our earthly work lay down,
And faith ne'er cease!

> Resurrection Sunday
> What did Jesus do on Sunday? Read the following scriptures to find out.
> Matthew 28:1-13   Mark 16:1-20   Luke 24:1-49   John 20:1-31

Easter Songs

Sing the two songs together as a family. Discuss what the songs mean. If you are not familiar with these songs, sing some Easter songs that you know (look in a hymnal for ideas).

All Hail the Power

Oliver Holden

1. All hail the pow'r of Jesus' name! Let angels prostrate fall;
   Bring forth the royal diadem, And crown Him Lord of all,
   Bring forth the royal diadem, And crown Him Lord of all!

2. Ye chosen seed of Israel's race, Ye ransomed from the fall,
   Hail Him who saves you by His grace, And crown Him Lord of all,
   Hail Him who saves you by His grace, And crown Him Lord of all!

3. Let ev'ry kindred, ev'ry tribe On this terrestrial ball,
   To Him all majesty ascribe, And crown Him Lord of all,
   To Him all majesty ascribe, And crown Him Lord of all! A-MEN.

Christ the Lord Is Risen Today

Countdown to Easter — 86 — Amy Puetz

INDEX

Authors
    Andersen, Hans Christian, 82
    Bailey, Carolyn Sherwin, 2, 27, 29
    Bailey, Temple, 75
    Cowles, Mrs. Julia, 49
    Kingsley, Florence Morse, 31
    Koudacheff, P. Kitty, 37, 44
    Levinger, Elma Ehrlich, 20
    Nash, Harriet A., 69
    Von Schmid, Christoph, 8, 14
    Wallace, Lew, 55, 62

Bible Reading
    Passion Week - Monday, 47
    Passion Week - Tuesday, 51
    Passion Week - Wednesday, 60
    Passion Week - Thursday, 67
    Passion Week - Good Friday, 73
    Resurrection Sunday, 85

Cooking
    Decorate Easter Eggs by Amy Puetz, 48
    Hot Cross Buns by Amy Puetz, 74
    Matzo Bread by Amy Puetz, 13

Crafts
    Easter Baskets by Amy Puetz, 30
    Easter Bookmarks by Amy Puetz, 41
    Easter Cards by Lina Beard and Adelia Belle Beard, 6
    Wall Hanging - History of the Passover by Amy Puetz, 23

Easter Chuckles by Melville De Lancey Landon & Mark Twain, 5
Easter Egg Activities—Easter Egg Hunt & The Celebration of Easter by Ellye Howell Glover, 52
Easter Egg Games by Lina Beard & Adelia Belle Beard, 53
Easter Party—Easter Hat Sale and Hoop Race for Easter by Ellye Howell Glover, 61
Easter Quiz—The Easter Story by Amy Puetz, 19
Easter Quiz—Who Said It? by Amy Puetz, 81
Easter Riddles by Melville De Lancey Landon & Mark Twain, 41
Easter—What is Easter? by William Tegg, 29
Experiment—An Egg-speriment—To Put an Egg in a Glass Bottle, 23

"How a Little Brown Bulb Became an Easter Lily" by Florence Ursula Palmer, 43

Legend of The Nails, 73

Poems
    "Easter Carol" by George Newell Lovejoy, 22
    "Easter Hymn" by Charles Wesley, 18
    "Easter Poem" by Caleb Davis Bradlee, 84
    "Jesus Christ is Risen Today" Author Unknown, 80
    "Luther's Easter Hymn," 7
    "Shadow of the Cross, The" by Horatius Bonar, 34
    "Splendor of the Lilies, The" by Margaret Elizabeth Munson Sangster, 40

Songs
    "Alas! And Did My Savior Bleed?" 35
    "All Hail the Power," 85
    "Beneath the Cross of Jesus," 68
    "Christ the Lord Is Risen Today," 86
    "Near the Cross," 36
    "When I Survey the Wondrous Cross," 67

Stories
    "Easter Eggs" by Christoph Von Schmid, 8, 14
    "Easter Snow Storm, An" by P. Kitty Koudacheff, 37, 44
    "Finding Easter" by Carolyn Sherwin Bailey, 2
    "General's Easter Box, The" by Temple Bailey, 75
    "Harold's Happy Easter" by Carolyn Sherwin Bailey, 28
    "Healer, The" by Lew Wallace, 62
    "Lesson of Faith, A" by Mrs. Julia Cowles, 49
    "Loveliest Rose in the World, The" by Hans Christian Andersen, 82
    "Love Triumphant" by Florence Morse Kingsley, 31
    "Miss Rebecca's Easter Blossoms" by Harriet A. Nash, 69
    "Nazarene, The" by Lew Wallace, 55
    "Playmates in Egypt" by Elma Ehrlich Levinger, 20
    "Wonder Egg, The" by Carolyn Sherwin Bailey, 29

"Two Thieves, The" by Mrs. Jameson, 47

Author Biography

Amy Puetz (pronounced Pitts) is a homeschool graduate, a self-taught historian, and a servant of Jesus Christ. History has been a passion for her since childhood. Years of in-depth study (both in modern and old sources) have equipped her to write history-related books. Amy Puetz is the author of *Uncover Exciting History: Revealing America's Christian Heritage in Short, Easy-to-Read Nuggets*. As a columnist for *Home School Enrichment Magazine* she shares stories about historical events from a Christian worldview. She especially loves to dig for little-known stories that show God's providential hand. Because of a chronic illness (fibromyalgia) that limits what she can do, the Lord led her to start an online business which she can do from home. She is the author of several e-books. In her spare time she enjoys sewing and reading. Visit her Web site at www.AmyPuetz.com to see many resources relating to history. She also publishes a bimonthly e-zine for ladies of all ages called *Heroines of the Past*.

www.AmyPuetz.com

Uncover Exciting History
Amy Puetz

Revealing America's Christian Heritage in Short, Easy-to-Read Nuggets

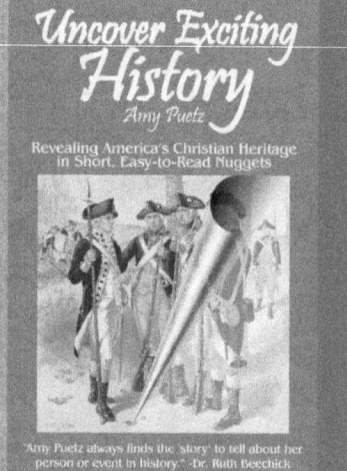

History Is Not Boring!

What is history anyway? It is the story of real people who did real things. For history to be fun for everyone (even those who think they hate history), it must go beyond hard facts and meaningless dates to the real people who made the significant events happen. People like George Washington, who bravely crossed the partly frozen Delaware River to attack the British at Trenton. Stories like that of the bold Americans who bravely fought against the Barbary pirates during the little-known Barbary War show how interesting history is.

True History Is Exciting!

Here are some of the stories in this book:
- Discover how the U.S. created the Constitution
- Experience the miraculous victory at the Battle of New Orleans
- Explore America's expansion west
- Uncover one of America's best weapons used during World War II

Each short, concise chapter is sure to delight students twelve and up, as well as adults who want a snapshot view of American history.

> "Amy Puetz always finds the 'story' to tell about her person or event in history." -Dr. Ruth Beechick
>
> "Story-telling is the greatest way to excite people about history, and Amy Puetz loves to tell stories. *Uncover Exciting History* is a great resource for Christian families and those who yearn to see God's hand behind American history." -Marcia Washburn
> Building Tomorrow's Generation at marciawashburn.com

Available at www.AmyPuetz.com

If you enjoyed this book you will also like Countdown to Christmas by Amy Puetz

Memory Making Stories and Activities for Every Day from December 1st to the 25th

Do you long to make this holiday season the best ever? Do you wish to escape from the commercialism that hounds us from every corner? Do you want to slow down this Christmas and enjoy the holiday as they did in the good old days?

If you answered yes to any of these questions, then I would like to offer you a wonderful book that will brighten your family's Christmas. *Countdown to Christmas* has family friendly stories and activities for every day from December 1st to the 25th. Imagine your family reading a Christmas story each day and then participating in a fun activity together. This will be made simple for you with *Countdown to Christmas*! The book is broken up into daily sections. Each day has a story and an activity that will take about 30 to 45 minutes.

Some of the stories included are:
"Becky's Christmas Dream" by Louisa May Alcott; "The Fir-Tree" by Hans Christian Andersen; "The Star" by Florence M. Kingsley; "The Conscience-Pudding" by E. Nesbit; "Why the Chimes Rang" by Raymond MacDonald Alden; "Christmas Every Day" by W.D. Howells; "Christmas Storms and Sunshine" by Elizabeth Gaskell.

Most of the stories in this book were written in the 1800s and early 1900s. Some of the language may seem old fashioned, but this only adds to their charm! Many of these stories have not been reprinted since their first publication, and are just waiting to be rediscovered by a whole new generation. *Countdown to Christmas* will appeal to any age group, but children ages 6-14 will enjoy it the most. Each story can be used to teach important lessons to your children. Reading aloud as a family will open up wonderful opportunities for discussions and conversations. The activities include: games, crafts, cooking, riddles, quizzes, singing carols, and more. This book will help families grow closer together.

> "Amy Puetz has created the warmth and joy of Christmas with her December 1-25 Christmas Countdown book. Her compiled classic stories, carols, and activities keep the family together and anticipating Christmas Day. With the busyness of the holiday season, this daily inspiration will warm your heart and keep your focus on the joy of Christmas. This book will be sure to make this year a Merry Christmas at your home!"
>
> Marcia Ramsland,
> author of *Simplify Your Holidays: A Classic Christmas Planner to Use Year after Year*

Make this Christmas truly memorable with Countdown to Christmas!
Available at www.AmyPuetz.com

Costumes With Character by Amy Puetz

Make Your Own Costumes from 11 Time Periods with 1 Dress!
Foreword by Mrs. Jennie Chancey

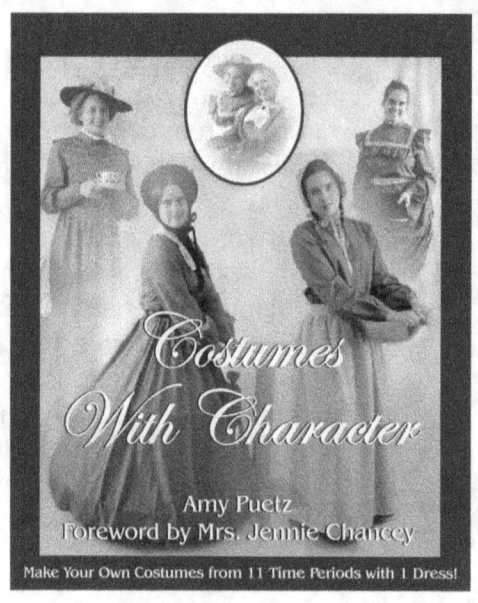

This exciting historical costume book has eleven creative costume patterns from the 1620s to the turn of the twentieth century (including Pilgrim, Puritan, Quaker, Revolutionary War, 1830s Pioneer, Civil War, two Victorian chapters, Turn of the Twentieth Century, and Sailor outfits), beautiful color photos, step-by-step easy-to-follow instructions, interesting facts about each time period, thought-provoking quotes by famous people, and a recommended resource reference chapter for further study.

"Amy's book made me excited about historical costumes again—costumes that I can easily make! I loved the simple instructions and helpful pictures." ~Nicole, age 16

"Costumes with Character is jam-packed with good things! Beautiful photos, patterns for your own use, historical tidbits, even how to give a tea party! With a full 3 pages of recommended classic reading and scripture throughout, this is definitely one you'll want for your homeschool library!" ~Elaine, homeschool mom

"This book is a true delight! It has a professional feel with detailed instructions but also many "extras" that reflect Amy's love of history including questions and quotes about each time period!" ~Connie, homeschool mom

Available at www.AmyPuetz.com

www.ingramcontent.com/pod-product-compliance
Lightning Source LLC
Chambersburg PA
CBHW051214290426
44109CB00021B/2447